GREAT INTERIORS

ENDPAPERS: *Design by Giuseppe Galli Bibiena (1696–1756) for a play performed at the nuptials of the Royal Prince of Poland, Prince Elector of Saxony*

GREAT INTERIORS

Edited by Ian Grant
Preface by Cecil Beaton
Photographs by Edwin Smith

Spring Books
London · New York · Sydney · Toronto

Original edition published 1967 and © 1967 by
George Weidenfeld and Nicolson Ltd, London,
and E.P. Dutton & Co., Inc., New York

This edition published 1971 by
The Hamlyn Publishing Group Limited
London · New York · Sydney · Toronto
Hamlyn House, Feltham, Middlesex, England

Printed in Italy by
Arnoldo Mondadori Editore Officine Grafiche,
Verona

ISBN 0 600 33882 7

CONTENTS

PREFACE

Cecil Beaton

We know that often the most noble architectural achievements have their roots in religious, social, or political foundations. But it is also true to say that the incentive which inspired many great buildings has been of a more individual nature. The glories of Versailles were created when the *Roi Soleil*, having seen Vaux-le-Vicomte, was determined to surpass Fouquet's splendours, and to prove to the world that the King of France was the most grandiose in all Europe. As a result, many other heads of countries – and in particular the small courts of Germany – were inspired to build their own fairy-tale Palaces; thus, out of motives of rivalry, the world's heritage is enriched.

But Louis was unique – a man of remarkable taste, flair, and knowledge. He knew how to frame his own flamboyant personality. His understanding of the arts and decoration was such that he was completely at ease with his architects, and on more sympathetic terms with his gardeners and artisans than with his nobles. Walking down mirror-lined corridors, past the silver furniture, the *tulipières*, and the orange trees, past the phalanxes of statues, he identified himself with the grandeur of his surroundings. The King himself must be the principal figure in the picture.

Most of us – according to our means – try to imprint our personality upon our surroundings. It is a human and a beneficial thing to do, for it is this tendency that has led to the creation of many rooms which give happiness. It is nearly always the personal that inspires and delights us; the pompous solemnity of Louis, the delicate femininity of Pompadour, the scholastic splendours of Marlborough, the wild fantasies of Ludwig of Bavaria, or even the cottagey cosiness of Norman Shaw.

When admiring these great interiors it is sometimes difficult to know how involved one's emotions become with one's aesthetic appreciation. Doubtless one is swayed by this historic association – by personal preferences for those responsible for creating, for living, or for dying, in these precious confines. We know that in the interiors that are completely satisfying, in those rooms that conjure up an atmosphere, that sing, that dance, our judgement is affected by whether the creator has managed successfully to say what he originally intended.

PREFACE

It is not easy to know to whom should go the greatest credit for these great monuments to individual taste. Is it to the architects, the decorators and painters, or do we allow full due to the formulators of taste? Decoration as we know of it today started with the Magnificent Lorenzo who more than anyone was responsible for the revival of interest in the arts and learning. Isabella d'Este, another great impresario-patron with feverish flair, sent out her emissaries from Mantua in every direction to buy treasures. But should we honour her, and others, Fouquet, Mazarin, Pompadour, and Burlington more than their architects?

Certainly without each other neither could succeed. Likewise we know that a whole world can divide the best intentions and the successful result.

There may be only a knife-edge difference between a room that is alive and one that has no soul. A replica may fail for lack of that elusive personal touch that only a virtuoso can give to the carving of a dragon, the stucco modelling of a bird, or a painted garland on a ceiling. We recognise the interior in which everything is in harmony – proportion, measure, ornamentation, furniture favourably placed, the choice of a personal object – and we can say of the result, as of a great painting or a piece of sculpture, that it can lay claim to be judged as a work of art.

Mr Ian Grant, and the distinguished scholars who have collaborated with him, have covered a wide field, and their choice of subjects is assured enough not to ignore Queen Mary's bedroom at Hampton Court while including such lesser known interiors as at Haga Slot. The choice is catholic in its contrasts, ranging from the Neo-Egyptian taste of Asplund in Sweden in the 1920s, the almost psychedelic swirls on floor and ceiling of the Gasparini Salon in Madrid's Royal Palace, the dining room at the Ritz Hotel in London, with its scallops of metal roses hanging from painted clouds, (undoubtedly the most beautiful Edwardian restaurant in existence), the sapphire satin upholstery of Queen Victoria's private railway train, and Whistler's Peacock Room in Washington, to Philip Johnson's *avant-garde* slumber room in Connecticut, with moving walls, dimming lights, and hidden music.

Their enthusiasm for the 'curiosities' such as Gaudí's Palacio Güell in Barcelona, the slate decorations of the absurdly ponderous Penrhyn Castle, or the cedar staircase at Harlaxton, is as great as for the Classic or Neo-classic colonnades and porticos at Chiswick, Caserta, Maisons-Lafitte, or Munich's National Theatre.

Of recent years the photography of great architecture has floundered between the Scylla of the super-technological and the Charybdis of the amateur snapshotter. With ever more highly sensitised film, and a greater accuracy of colour emulsion, architectural photographs, particularly in France, Germany, and the United States, have become so precise that one can discern with equal clarity, and with scarcely little difference of emphasis, the bowl of fruit in the foreground and the brick on the farthest horizon. The antiseptic quality of the results is apt to rob the subject of its shadows, its patina, and its innate personality, particularly when flash and strobe, and other artificial means of lighting are used. In contrast the work produced by young photographers with their hand-held cameras has introduced us to pictures that are violent in juxtaposition of light and shade, or great distortions, and often of a Samsonesque effect, not necessarily intended, of columns falling inwards. An egg-cup or silver canister, by being placed so near the lens, is given more importance than the distant triumphal arch. The effects are all very atmospheric and in the contemporary mood, but they often result in a lack of detail and a falsity in the tonality.

Perhaps the photographing of so essentially static a subject as architecture is the least suitable to be essayed by the candid camera (which is presumably aimed at catching the bird or butterfly on the wing). To bring these interiors to life takes great knowledge, not only in the sense of knowing how to compose the whole as a picture, or in lighting and exposure, but in the later technical processes (of printing and developing) whereby all values are given to contrasting surfaces.

Three-quarters of the photographs in this book are the work of someone with that great knowledge, who, having trained as an architect, is an understanding and loving connoisseur of his subject. He talks of each photographic session as 'an act of admiration'. Edwin Smith's photographs are a happy mean between the two schools of architectural photography. Though appreciative of the cool, calm, and beautifully controlled photographs beloved of *Country Life*, he has also a mastery over dramatising the composition; for making the significant detail loom large in the foreground. He appreciates the elusive effects of dark shadows on sculptural giants, or of sunlight filtering through the clouds on to the plaster *putti* flying among arabesques of ribbon, or on to some glorious golden goddess caressing her naked body. But although drama is here, there are no shortcuts to effect, no clumsy mis-uses of horizontals, no accidentally falling columns or tottering towers. Even in black and white he is able to suggest the richness of the dark Christmas-pudding panelling below the brandy-butter stucco ceilings of English country houses, the delicate spirals of the wood carving at Chatsworth, Belton, or Petworth. In his colour plates the flying figures with their burdens of drapery on the ceiling of the state bedroom at Vaux-le-Vicomte sparkle with gold leaf.

Edwin Smith is a photographer after my own heart. Travelling without an assistant or even a light metre, he merely brings to each job his understanding of architecture, his enthusiasm and his artistry. He enjoys the 'gorgeous' risk of returning from a long and strenuous voyage abroad with all his undeveloped film in one basket. Often he is delighted to discover that with his use of long exposures, and by screening the lens from light, final prints reveal details that had eluded him, that the camera can pick out things that we cannot see for ourselves.

To turn these pages is to be presented with the key to rooms that give wing to the imagination, that illuminate the mind. For many of us it will be the only opportunity of visiting these distant and diverse places. For such a magic carpet expedition we are very much indebted to all who have contributed to this richly filled book.

INTRODUCTION

Ian Grant

The guiding principle behind this selection of great interiors has been a search for a quality best defined as unity, and this seems to have three principal constituent factors. The greatest rooms may show any of these factors together in innumerable variations.

The most impressive unity is that which is achieved by a closely considered and fully developed architectural theme, moulding internal volume into reverse sculpture, drawing together the elements of structure, joinery and cabinet work into carefully related harmonies and absorbing applied decoration and furniture into an indivisible amalgam. This type of interior is necessarily of the rarest sort, for its execution demands skill of the highest order; nevertheless, an inspiringly large number do exist, as a visit to Prince Eugene's palace in Vienna, or Raconigi, or St Catherine's College, Oxford, will show.

A second kind of unity, not as powerful as the first, but still possessing important qualities, is that achieved by a closely related and complete scheme of furniture and moveable decoration. This may have been introduced into a room that has little relation to it, or which even has a character which is at variance to it. In spite of this, the *mobilier* (as in the 'Briar Rose' room at Buscot), can have sufficient dominance for a perfect balance to be achieved.

The last kind of unity is that which is brought about by the use of colour. In some ways this is the most interesting, since colour is perhaps the most stimulating of all the components which go to make up an interior, and when skilfully used, it can successfully co-ordinate otherwise unrelated elements, like those in Whistler's Peacock Room.

Stringently though principles of selection may be applied, in the final reckoning the number of examples that can be included far exceeds the space available, and it is at this point that the personalities of the selectors become evident: the reader will soon detect a preference for the classical rather than the romantic, for the bold rather than the restrained, for the grand rather than the cosy.

It is to be hoped, however, that the examples chosen will please when they introduce enthusiasts to hitherto unknown architectural delights, or when they remind them of excitements they had forgotten.

EARLY CLASSICAL
1650-1700

Ralph Dutton

In tracing the development of the Renaissance as it affected domestic architecture in the principal countries of Europe during the second half of the seventeenth century it seems logical to start with Italy, which led the movement, and then to move northwards to France. In the countries of central Europe this was not a fertile period, but geographically it seems best to glance at the buildings there, before passing on to the Netherlands, and so crossing the Channel to England where, once the Restoration was accomplished, a strong wave of building started which was to continue for a century or more. This, then, is the plan of the following chapter.

Italy John Ruskin ends *The Stones of Venice* with a chapter on Renaissance architecture. This he divides into three sections: Early, Roman, and Grotesque. For the first two he reluctantly finds some faint praise, but on the final phase – the phase we would now call Baroque – he heaps vituperation of the most violent description, and attributes its corrupt elements to 'pride and infidelity'. 'The architecture raised during this period', he thundered, 'is among the worst and basest ever built'; and as he floated down the Grand Canal in his gondola he must have shuddered as he passed examples of the 'basest' style such as the majestic façade of the Palazzo Pesaro which was begun by Baldassare Longhena in 1663.

It is interesting to compare Ruskin's views with those of the Baroque architect Guarino Guarini who wrote his *Architettura civile* in the third quarter of the seventeenth century. In Guarini's view Gothic builders aimed at erecting structures of such lightness that it seemed miraculous that stone vaults could be supported on such slender shafts and above walls pierced by spacious windows. 'Vaults without the support of walls', he wrote, explaining the objective of Gothic builders as he saw it. The Classical style, on the other hand, aimed at creating a sense of massive strength so that a building would impose by its solidity. However, he was without the bigotry of Ruskin, and admitted that both styles – although basically so opposed – had much to recommend them.

opposite. The dining room, Belton House, near Grantham, Lincolnshire, England. All the elements that make up the special atmosphere of the English seventeenth-century interior are gathered together in this room. The house was completed in 1689

EARLY CLASSICAL

It is doubtful whether many of Ruskin's contemporaries held equally violent views, but for many years Baroque architecture remained under a dark cloud of disapprobation, and guide books were inclined to dismiss the finest examples of the style in a few scathing words. Now, a century or so after Ruskin was fulminating, Baroque architecture has emerged into the sunshine again, and without any sense of defending an unpopular cause, one can praise the buildings which were erected in Europe during the half century which is covered by this chapter.

The Renaissance style developed early in Italy – the noble buildings of Palladio belong to the sixteenth century – but beyond the Alps, in France, in central Europe, and in far away England, the style was slow to take root largely owing to the fact that in all these countries artistic impulses were stultified by political and religious turmoil, covering decades which should otherwise have been fruitful for the arts. Thus it came about that in these regions architecture was enjoying a slightly retarded blossoming at a time when in Italy it was beginning to move slowly down the gentle slope of decadence.

At the turn of the seventeenth century, however, Italy, and particularly Rome, still held its proud position as the artistic centre of Europe, and a city which contained two men of such eminence in their profession as Gianlorenzo Bernini and Francesco Borromini could hardly have been anything but the fountainhead to which all architects looked for inspiration. As the century was ending, however, the situation changed. For a young architect it was still looked upon as the finest training to spend a few years in Italy, but it was in order to study the architecture of ancient Rome and the works of Palladio, and not contemporary buildings.

Bernini (1598–1680) was one of those universal geniuses who appeared from time to time in Italy, and was only surpassed in the breadth of his talents and attainments by Michelangelo. He was architect, sculptor and painter, though the last profession was somewhat neglected in face of his intense activity in the two first. On a number of occasions in history a great genius has appeared at a time when there is a splendid opportunity for him to show his talent. In England, for example, Christopher Wren burst onto the architectural scene when the City of London had to be rebuilt after the Great Fire. Thus in Rome, Bernini was available to carry out the lavish projects of three successive popes, Urban VIII, Innocent X and Alexander VII, covering between them the years 1623 to 1667, and under whose reigns the whole face of Rome was changed.

Bernini's work was primarily ecclesiastical, but he designed several *palazzi* for great families, such as the Montecitorio and the Chigi, but these, now turned to public use, have been so much altered, particularly in their interiors, that there is nothing to show how Bernini decorated the rooms behind his magnificent façades. In the Palazzo Barberini, however, many of the rooms still retain their original decoration, and although dating from a decade before the turn of the century, they provide an example of the embellishment of a Bernini *palazzo*.

This vast palace, standing on the slope of the hill near the Quattro Fontane, was begun by the architect Maderna, but after his death the work was carried on from 1631 by Bernini with the assistance of Borromini. The decoration of the Gran Salone, on the

piano nobile, which must date from shortly before 1650, remains as originally designed. It is a huge room of great height, with a deeply coved ceiling above a projecting cornice. On the cove Pietro da Cortona painted a glorification of the reign of Urban VIII, the Barberini pope, in the style of the most exuberant Baroque. In an architectural framework painted to simulate stucco, quantities of figures float upwards towards Divine Providence who is seated in a blaze of light on a cloud, while in another part of this highly populated Olympus the Barberini bees, the family emblem, appear within a wreath supported by flying maidens. Although the theme of the painting may seem rather absurd, the effect achieved is one of the utmost magnificence.

Borromini's domestic work was more extensive than Bernini's, and his buildings were inclined to show greater fantasy. This tendency was shown principally in the façades, with which we are not here concerned; but in the court of the Palazzo Spada he created a *trompe-l'oeil* effect which rivals that of Palladio in the Teatro Olimpico at Vicenza. By an ingenious arrangement of a series of diminishing columns and arches he created the perspective of a long gallery within an actual length of no more than a few feet.

A room more typical of the period is the great gallery on the first floor of the Palazzo Colonna. It was begun from designs of Antonio del Grande in 1654, but was not completed till twenty years later, when the ceiling was painted by Coli and Gherardi with a spirited scene representing the naval battle of Lepanto of 1571. Here again the central scene is surrounded by an architectural framework painted to represent stucco, the rigidity of which is broken by garlands and figures. The walls of the room are largely plain and on them is hung the great family collection of pictures.

EARLY CLASSICAL

opposite. *A detail of the ceiling of the state bedroom, Château de Vaux-le-Vicomte, France, designed by Le Vau and built between 1657 and 1661 for Nicholas Fouquet, finance minister to Louis XIV. Shortly after the completion of his house, Fouquet fell from favour, but not, as legend has it, because of the King's jealousy of the grandeur of his house*

Both the Barberini and the Colonna rooms are firmly rectangular in form and show none of that fluidity of planning which, as we shall see, became so outstanding a feature of French domestic architecture. They were designed, it would seem, to form suitable fields for the contemporary artists to cover with their sumptuous paintings with the minimum of interference of architectural detail and decoration.

It was not only in Rome that the Baroque style was flourishing during the second half of the seventeenth century; in Venice, under the aegis of Baldassare Longhena, a number of splendid buildings arose. Indeed in Rome Bernini found his talents neglected during the last decade of his life, which ended in 1680, as support from the Papacy diminished, but in Venice Longhena was carrying out commissions for the rich patricians until his death two years after Bernini. It can hardly be said of Longhena that he altered the face of Venice, as it was of Bernini at Rome, but his structures unquestionably add greatly to the splendour of the city, while his church of Santa Maria della Salute epitomises the spirit of Venice perhaps more strongly than any other building.

Longhena's domestic work is seen at its best in the façade of the Ca'Pesaro, but this elaborate Baroque frontage conceals rooms which are austerely plain. It was intended no doubt that the walls should be hung with tapestries, and for this reason the decoration was confined to paintings on the coved ceilings, and to some simply sculptured doorways.

An unaltered example of an interior in a building designed by Longhena can be seen in the Sala dell'Archivio in the Scuola Grande dei Carmini of 1668. The walls are lined for a third of their height with massive wainscoting with caryatids between the panels. The wall space above is completely covered by large canvasses and the bold cornice is in unpainted wood as is the elaborately carved ceiling into which Menescardi pictures are set.

In Turin also there was great architectural activity during the half century under review. The Palazzo Reale, a building of huge size but of uninspired elevation, was begun by Castellamonte for Carlo Emmanuel II in 1658, but the elaborate decoration of the interior dates from the following century. The most accomplished architect working in Turin at this period was Guarino Guarini, whose writings have already been mentioned. His works were principally ecclesiastical, but the Palazzo Carignano, with a Baroque façade in brick – an unusual combination – is one of his rare domestic buildings and dates from 1679.

France

During the reign of Louis XIV (1643–1715) France, which had been backward in culture compared to Italy, showed a remarkable advance, and one can agree with Voltaire when he wrote in 1776:

Although Henry IV may have been a great man, his era was not great in any way … The arts of peace, which form the charm of society, which beautify cities, which illuminate the mind, which civilise manners: all these began only in the age in which Louis XIV was born and died.

This golden era, however, started slowly, at least in the direction of domestic architecture, for the King followed the policy of Richelieu in weakening the power of the

16

nobility, and to this end he ordered the destruction of châteaux in the country which might be able to offer resistance to the royal forces. The Fronde was not quickly forgotten. But in 1661 Richelieu died, and his protégé, Colbert, succeeded him in his offices and held them till his death twenty-two years later.

The new minister was as ardent a builder as the King himself, and it is possible that without Colbert's encouragement in his early life Louis' enthusiasm for constructing palaces and laying out gardens might not have developed into the passion which almost ruined the country; but which has left the monuments which now provide pleasure for millions.

With great astuteness Colbert gathered the foremost practitioners of the visual arts into the royal service and thus was able to advance his plan for the glorification of the monarchy. But before Colbert removed the greater part of the available talent out of the reach of private individuals, a few splendid châteaux had been built in the Ile-de-France by men who had special opportunities for acquiring wealth. In 1642 Réné de Longueil, a cunning financier and politician, commissioned François Mansart to build a magnificent house at Maisons on the edge of the Forest of Saint-Germain, and this château, in spite of many vicissitudes, remains one of the finest productions of the period. Since the decoration of the interior seems to have been completed at the turn of the century, it merits inclusion here. The planning shows a subtlety never seen in earlier houses, while the richness and nobility of the decoration seems to have been based on the best Italian Renaissance style. The entrance vestibule with Doric pillars and pilasters, supporting a coved ceiling richly carved in stone, leads to a robust stone stair which mounts in three flights to the first floor. This fine but reserved architecture compares highly favourably with the richness and splendour of decoration which was about to become popular.

An example of the ornate style is the Château of Vaux-le-Vicomte, near Melun, which Louis Le Vau designed for Fouquet, the *Surintendant des Finances*, in 1657. The story of the owner's incarceration as soon as the house had been completed is too well-known to be repeated, but before this unhappy event the combined genius of Le Vau in the house and Le Nôtre in the garden had produced the most magnificent *ensemble* ever created by a private individual in France – or perhaps in the world. In the decoration of the interior Le Vau had the assistance of Lebrun, who was to become one of the principal lights of the royal circle of talent, and it is strongly Italian in feeling. The most spectacular room is that designed for the King who was to encompass Fouquet's downfall. It is embellished with all the richness which plaster decoration, gilding and painting could produce; the principal elaboration is on the coved ceiling where flying figures, *putti* and a wealth of wreaths and swags surround Lebrun's paintings.

Having lodged Fouquet safely in gaol, the King and Colbert transferred all the brilliant band of craftsmen into the royal service, prudently adding to their number the major-domo, the famous Vatel. From this time forward the most elaborate, but not necessarily the most beautiful, decoration is to be found in the royal palaces, or occasionally in the houses of those closely connected with the Court. Thus France is the reverse of England, where the work in the great country houses is in general finer than that in the palaces.

Colbert's intention was to solidify the monarchy by housing the young King in

opposite. First-floor salon, Château de Balleroy, near Bayeux, France. Decorated like a miniature Versailles, the wood of the doorways and the plastered walls are painted to imitate marble. The large painting by Mignard shows Madame de Montespan and her children. François Mansart completed the structure in 1636, and decoration went on inside for many years

splendour in his capital, and to this end he turned his attention to completing the work which had already been begun on the Louvre. The dissentions which occurred over the building of the great east façade need not be told here, but of more interest was the decoration of the Galerie d'Apollon which Le Vau and Lebrun were commissioned to undertake in 1663. This magnificent room on the first floor is 200 feet in length and is embellished with the same richness of plasterwork, gilding and painting which the architects and their craftsmen had used at Vaux. The nineteenth century, however, has laid its hand on this room, and the panels of Gobelins tapestry set into the plasterwork date from this period.

Colbert's plan to attract Louis to the Louvre was a failure, for the King's heart was at the château which his father had built at Versailles in the forests to the west of Paris, and it was here, and in the smaller palaces he erected in its neighbourhood, that the greater part of his life was spent. Colbert must have realised the failure of his plan when the King ordered the band of architects and decorators to convert the country house into a magnificent palace, and Le Nôtre to mould the marshy surroundings into a layout even more extensive and splendid than that at Vaux.

Several of the *Grands Appartements* still exist basically as Le Vau designed them before his death in 1670. The Salle des Gardes de la Reine has the walls divided into large panels inlaid with marbles of various colours, while from the cornice springs a coved ceiling on which are paintings set in gilded plaster frames. In both the style of the façades and in the ornamentation of the rooms there was more than an echo of contemporary Italian design, but Le Vau and Lebrun here provided their own rendering of the Italian theme.

The King's passion for building was not appeased by these works, and after the Peace of Nijmegen in 1678 he commanded Jules Hardouin-Mansart, the brilliant nephew of François Mansart, to convert Versailles into the largest palace in the world. Thus the long lateral wings were added and the Galerie des Glaces with the Salon de la Guerre and Salon de la Paix at either end were created, facing over the gardens. The gallery with its seventeen arch-topped windows, which are repeated by mirrors on the opposite wall, and marble pilasters supporting the deep cornice below the coved ceiling, is of the greatest possible magnificence, but the decoration of the end rooms shows greater originality, and of these the Salon de la Guerre is the more impressive. The walls are lined with panels of coloured marbles on which are gilded trophies, while above the bolection moulding of the fire opening is a vast oval relief in plaster by Coysevox of Louis XIV on his charger trampling vanquished enemies.

Much more could be written about the decoration of rooms at Versailles dating from this period, but it is equally important to glance at the work in the houses of private individuals, although it is more modest than that produced by the unlimited royal extravangance.

A number of the rich nobility erected large houses in Paris during the second half of the seventeenth century, and the ingenuity of architects in utilising to the best effect an awkwardly shaped site was remarkable. They showed a resource and a fertility of ideas far in advance of contemporary work in England. The general plan, which became almost a convention, though it was infinitely varied, consisted of a block on the street containing

A Lady at her toilet *by Jan Steen. This charming domestic scene shows, in minute detail, the simple and attractive furnishing of a bourgeois interior of the mid-seventeenth century, and the architectural framing demonstrates the enthusiasm for Classical decoration which was exciting all Europe at this time*

domestic offices, through which an archway opened into a court with the main building on the far side and a garden beyond. The charm of these ranges *entre cour et jardin*, where they survive, is great, and the planning was often extremely effective.

One of the most attractive built at this period is the Hôtel Lambert on the eastern point of the Ile Saint-Louis. Le Vau was the architect and work was begun in 1640, but the decoration by Lebrun and Le Sueur was carried on for more than a decade. The most important room is the Galerie d'Hercule on the first floor. It is over seventy feet in length with five windows looking onto the garden and three in the apse-shaped end facing up the river. On the ceiling are paintings by Lebrun, and on the walls carved reliefs by Van Obstal representing the labours of Hercules.

A short way from the Hôtel Lambert on the same quay is the Hôtel Lauzun which forms an interesting contrast to the former. Although begun seventeen years later, it is less sophisticated both in planning and decoration than the building created by Le Vau and his assistant. The name of the architect is unknown, but it was already completed when it was bought by the Duc de Lauzun, the boisterous character who married La Grande Mademoiselle and spent twelve years of his life in the Bastille for being a nuisance to Louis XIV. The interest of the hôtel lies in the elaborate gilded panelling which lines four rooms on the second floor. Pilasters, swags, urns in relief, inset pictures – mostly landscapes – topped by richly carved cornices below coved and painted ceilings produce an effect of tremendous splendour, an effect indeed – since the rooms are not very large – which is almost overwhelming. Although the detail is extremely fine, the design lacks the discipline found in the work of Le Vau and Lebrun which stemmed from their knowledge of Italian work.

Decoration so ornate can rarely have been executed outside Paris, but similar rooms exist in at least two country châteaux. Within the austere walls of the Château de Cormatin, in the department of Saône-et-Loire, are two suites of rooms, known as Les Salles Dorées, where the decoration is even more exuberant than in the Hôtel Lauzun in that not only the walls but also the ceilings are encrusted with the richest carving. One of these rooms, la Salle de Sainte-Cécile, is said to be the work of Pierre Puget, but there would seem to be nothing except the date (*c.* 1665) to suggest that this was probable.

The other house where similar work is to be found is the romantic Château d'Oiron, fifteen miles south of Chinon. The rooms are contained within the seventeenth-century fabric which was built on a grand scale. The two main rooms were designed to be hung with tapestry so that the riotous decoration is confined to the chimney breasts and to the ceiling. The beams are encrusted with swags of fruit and foliage amongst which cherubs float about roundels designed to contain paintings. Some of this abundant decoration is carried out in papiermâché and some is carved in oak, but all is brilliantly painted with deep blue and gold predominating. Adjacent to these rather barbaric rooms is the little Cabinet des Muses, where the decoration is more subtle and restrained. A deep moulding surrounds the room, dividing the walls into roughly equal parts; the lower half is decorated with oval panels in gilded frames painted with exotic trees, with pendant swags hanging between them. In the upper part pairs of fluted pillars coloured blue and white rise between paintings of the Muses.

This was the château which was bought by Madame de Montespan after losing the favour of Louis XIV, and where she spent the last years of her life.

Central Europe

The intense activity which was in progress in France in the development of the visual arts during the second half of the seventeenth century affected directly, but unevenly, the architecture of central Europe; for, although Italy remained the prime source for study of the arts, France was becoming the shining example of their fruition. Central Europe was made up of a complex of states which, even if not actually at war with each other, were generally bitterly opposed; and although Vienna was the centre of major Catholic power, its influence did not extend into the Protestant areas to the north. The Thirty Years' War raged over this region and brought widespread devastation and poverty. Under these conditions the civilised arts which had flourished before its outbreak were completely stifled. The Peace of Westphalia in 1648 brought this miserable strife to an end.

There remained, however, the menace of the Turks and it was not until the last years of the seventeenth century that, having been defeated in their siege of Vienna in 1682, they were finally driven out of Hungary and Transylvania by the victory of Prince Eugene at the battle of Zenta in 1697.

As a result of these highly disturbing events, central Europe is not rich in architecture of the second half of the seventeenth century, but during the last decade foreign practitioners of the visual arts came to work in these countries and found a profitable field for their productions. As Professor Eberhard Hempel points out in his *Baroque Art and Architecture in Central Europe*, the Baroque style came to these countries a century after it

had first developed in Italy, and then blossomed in a very specialised form – a form very different from that in any other country. Once having gained a foothold in the years following 1680 it flourished exceedingly until after seventy years or so of popularity it merged into Rococo.

It must not be supposed that architecture in Vienna was at a standstill during the years of turmoil, but building was principally ecclesiastical, and conditions were little conducive to the erection of large private houses. Nevertheless Leopold I was able to add a great new façade to the Hofburg between 1661 and 1668, and the Staremberg Palace, a massive building five stories high like the Hofburg, was begun in the same year. Out in the countryside a number of abbeys were erected towards the end of the century, in which the lavish plasterwork of the Carlone family was the outstanding feature, but these buildings, although setting a trend in style, do not qualify for inclusion here.

In Bohemia and Moravia the effects of the war had been less severe, and many of the great families had managed during this period to add to their wealth and estates. Thus when peace eventually came to their quarrelling neighbours they were in a highly favourable position for enlarging their country houses or for building majestic palaces in the capital. The vast Cernin Palace in Prague, which was begun in 1668, shows the happy financial condition of that family two decades after the end of the Thirty Years' War.

The dominating figure in the architectural sphere during the last quarter of the seventeenth century was Fischer von Erlach who had trained in Rome and had seen the buildings of Bernini and Borromini. It was, however, a restrained version of Baroque that he practised in the many buildings which he designed in Austria, and it was grouping and proportion rather than lavish decoration with which he achieved his effects. In interior decoration, however, he allowed greater elaboration, and in the huge oval hall at Schloss

EARLY CLASSICAL

Vranov in Moravia which was built from 1690–4 he produced a sumptuous *ensemble*. Corinthian pilasters, between which stand statutes in niches, support a deep freize and cornice, and above it the coved ceiling is painted with celestial scenes and *trompe l'oeil* sculpture. It is inevitably reminiscent of Le Vau's oval salon at Vaux-le-Vicomte which dates from more than thirty years earlier, and provides a striking example of the time-lag between France and Austria. A number of painters and craftsmen came at this period to Austria where there was an increasing demand for their work, and the style of ceilings which Fischer von Erlach favoured gave splendid opportunities to artists. He largely abandoned the type subdivided by plasterwork into small panels containing painted canvases, and instead covered his churches and his rooms with coves or shallow domes on which an artist could paint a spreading composition and so achieve a scene of recession and depth.

Although many of the practitioners of the visual arts came from north Italy at this period, an indigenous style practised by the artists of the country soon developed, so that by the end of the seventeenth century the Baroque of southern Germany and Austria was an established style. It differed from that of Italy, though both were highly theatrical. It might be said that Baroque in Italy was sombre drama, in Germany exciting comedy: the former was designed to impress by strength and gloom, the latter to stimulate by its gaiety.

These tendencies are principally to be seen in the ecclesiastical buildings for which southern Germany and Austria are famous, and which far outshine any domestic building. Several palaces, however, were begun during the last years of the century, but little of the original decoration survives. Fischer began Schönbrunn on the outskirts of Vienna for Joseph I but his work is now obscured by subsequent alterations. In 1697 Lukas von Hildebrandt built the Schwarzenberg Palace which now, with the spread of the town, seems almost in the centre of Vienna, but his superb Belvedere palaces come a little too late for this chapter. The latter were the summer residences of the national hero, Prince Eugene, but his Winter Palace in the town was begun in 1695 by Fischer, and the entrance hall with its four muscular caryatids is one of the triumphs of Austrian Baroque. The virility of the carving and austere nature of the decoration seem designed as a suitable setting for this remarkable man who, although unimpressive in person, was endowed with a brilliant intellect and a body inured to physical hardship.

Bavaria at this period remained far behind Austria in the development of its architecture, largely due to the effects of the War of the Spanish Succession in which the Elector Max Emmanuel imprudently joined the losing side, and was exiled for a decade from his country. However, before this disaster descended on him he had, while still a young man of twenty-one, engaged the Italian architect Enrico Zuccalli to rebuild the Palace of Schleissheim, a few miles from Munich. Work began in 1684 on a banqueting pavilion, a pavilion on a grandiose scale, in the grounds of the palace and facing the façade across an expanse of grass and water. Lustheim, as it is called, contains a two-storied central salon frescoed by Giovanni Turbiglio, so that as an interior it is an example of Italian rather than of Bavarian Baroque.

A picture gallery *by Jan Francken. This picture, painted during the second quarter of the seventeenth century, reflects the intellectual climate of the time. This was the period when the formation of private collections of works of art became extremely fashionable*

Holland

It is with some relief that one leaves the complexities of central Europe for the clearer situation in the Netherlands. Here the general surge upwards during the seventeenth century was a remarkable phenomenon, and the success of this small country in both naval and military spheres was astonishing. The Spanish domination was finally thrown off, and the Dutch navy carried out several successful engagements against the Spanish and British navies. But it is primarily for the extraordinary achievements of their artists that the seventeenth is known as 'The Great Century'. Franz Hals, followed by Rembrandt and a host of other painters, formed a school of painting rivalled only by Italy. Their style was their own, and it was not until the following century that Dutch artists studied in Italy, and returned to their own country to paint Italian landscapes peopled with Dutch figures.

Domestic architecture in the Netherlands had a style as strongly indigenous as painting. Throughout the seventeenth century comfortable brick houses with dignified and reticent façades were built in The Hague and along the canals of Amsterdam, Utrecht and other towns by prosperous merchants and rich landowners. The Mauritshuis, in The Hague, begun in 1633, is one of the finest houses of this type and, although the design suggests that the architect Jacob van Campen had studied contemporary Italian buildings, it is essentially Dutch in feeling. The average house built during the second half of the century was far less ambitious and usually presented to the passer-by a plain brick front with an orderly arrangement of windows. But surprisingly some of these simple façades concealed interiors decorated with plasterwork almost as exuberant as anything to be found in France at the time. This elaborate ornamentation was due to the vogue created by that fertile craftsman and designer Daniel Marot. Marot was a Huguenot, born in Paris in 1650, where he had his early training, and he came to Holland at the time of the persecutions. He carried out work for William of Orange and followed him to England where he designated himself on his drawings '*Architecte de sa Majesté Britanicque*'. He made many rather florid designs for the embellishment of rooms at Hampton Court which Wren was building for William and Mary, and it was rather as a decorator than as an architect that he excelled. He based his designs on the style in vogue in France at the time of his departure, but added to it a heavy elaboration which was out of keeping with contemporary French taste. Furniture, for which he made a great quantity of drawings, some of which were carried out and still exist, was remarkable more for its richness than for its purity of line.

The most famous surviving room created by Daniel Marot, perhaps with the aid of his son who had the same name, is the Trèves Zaal in the Binnenhof Palace at The Hague, which dates from 1697. Pilasters support a modillioned cornice from which springs a deep cove divided into panels by caryatids which appear to hold up the flat of the ceiling. All above the cornice is covered with frescoes while the walls are predominantly white and gold. The effect is sumptuous. At Lange Vyverberg 8, in the same town, a rich patrician's house, Marot used much the same elements in the upper hall; but here the cove of the ceiling is covered with rich plasterwork while over the doorways are busts set in niches.

But these are not the style of interiors which are familiar to us from the painters of 'The Great Century': they differ fundamentally from the rather prophylactic rooms which were painted by masters such as Pieter de Hooch or Vermeer. In these we see the black and white marble floors, the beamed unplastered ceilings, the plain walls hung with a few pictures, and tall lattice windows through which a shaft of sunshine may fall on a table covered with a rug. It is rooms such as these which were typical of the second half of the seventeenth century, and not the grand halls produced by the Marots, but it is the magnificent rather than the simple which has survived.

England

opposite. *The Cabal room, Ham House, England. Magnificent silk-on-wool tapestries by Bradshaw, from the Soho manufactury, cover the walls above the wainscot. They were made during the years from 1730 to 1750 and show scenes from Watteau. The room itself, with a richly moulded plaster ceiling, dates from around 1675*

The parentage of English domestic architecture in the seventeenth century has been said to be by Italy out of Holland, but there is no more than a partial truth in this. During the first half of the century a number of country houses – Raynham, Swakeleys, the Dutch House at Kew, for example – were built which show very strongly the influence of the Dutch Renaissance, but simultaneously Inigo Jones was erecting buildings of the purest Italian lineage. The outbreak of the Civil War and the following austere régime of the Commonwealth frustrated the development of architectural style, and this pause of nearly twenty years must have robbed England of many interesting buildings.

Work, however, was not entirely at a standstill, and it was the pure style of Inigo Jones which found favour with the few who were bold enough to build or embellish their country houses during the Commonwealth, and not, as might have been expected, the simpler Dutch manner. It is remarkable that at this singularly barren period one of the most splendid rooms in England should have been created. This is the Double Cube

Room at Wilton, which was built for the fifth Earl of Pembroke, who was one of Cromwell's supporters.

The house was severely damaged by fire in 1647 or 1648, and Lord Pembroke called in Inigo Jones and his pupil John Webb to restore the interior. Jones was then seventy-four years old and within five years of his death, so that at least the execution of the work, if not the design, must be attributed to the younger man. The dimensions are sixty feet in length by thirty feet wide and high, but the appearance of height is reduced by a massive cornice set some nine feet below the ceiling level, from which springs a deep cove painted with vases, wreaths and sculptured ornaments by Edward Pierce, while on the central panels are allegorical scenes of the sort which were to come into favour later in the century. The decoration of the walls was designed to take the full-length portraits by Van Dyke, and between these hang pendant swags of fruit and foliage in carved wood which still bear their original gilding.

After Inigo Jones's death, Webb received several commissions for rebuilding, or improving country houses, but little of his internal work survives. Ashburnham House in Westminster, which was built in 1662, is attributed to him on slender evidence. The staircase is effective and cleverly planned, but the detail seems hardly of the quality of Webb's work.

A more accomplished architect than Webb was Sir Roger Pratt, who was clearly an ardent admirer of Jones's work. Until a few years ago a room from Coleshill, in Berkshire, would certainly have been included in this book but in 1952 the house was gutted by fire and subsequently demolished. His houses, indeed, have been singularly unfortunate. Kingston Lacy and his own house of Ryston in Norfolk have been much altered, and the magnificent house he built for Lord Clarendon soon after the Restoration was demolished fifteen years later. Rather similar in general design to Clarendon House is Belton in Lincolnshire; no architect's name is attached to it – although the names of a number of craftsmen are known – but it was certainly not Pratt for it was only begun in 1684, the year of his death. Indeed Clarendon House seems to have formed the model for several country houses erected during the wave of building which followed the Restoration.

Belton contains some of the most beautiful Stuart rooms in England in which magnificence and intimacy are admirably mingled. The walls of the principal rooms are lined with large moulded panels topped by finely carved cornices which echo the crisp plasterwork of the ceilings. But the most important feature of these rooms is the carving, the superb swags and wreaths of flowers, fruit, leaves, birds, fishes and all manner of other motifs carved with an airy lightness and grace by the incomparable Grinling Gibbons. Until this period carving had inclined to solidity, as in the swags at Wilton, but Gibbons transformed the art, and his exquisite festoons are almost as fine and delicate as the petals and leaves produced by Nature herself.

Perhaps the most famous room which Gibbons embellished is the Carved Room at Petworth which he carried out for the Duke of Somerset in the years following 1689. The walls are lined with oak and on this plain background hang Gibbons's superb decorations carved in the soft but tough wood of the lime tree. His wreaths surround, and in some cases marry into pairs, the full-length portraits which hang on the walls, and

Opposite. The ceiling of the ante-room, Prince Eugene's Winter Palace, Vienna. Here are assembled all the elements of the full flood of Austrian Baroque decoration at the turn of the seventeenth and eighteenth centuries

show an astounding fertility of imagination as well as an extreme delicacy in execution.

The success of Gibbons's carvings started a vogue, and there were soon other talented craftsmen who carried out admirable work, though none quite equalled the master. In the imposing suite of rooms which Talman designed for the first Duke of Devonshire at Chatsworth between the years 1687 and 1696, Samuel Watson, a young man in his twenties and a native of Derbyshire, ornamented the panelled walls with carving of the greatest richness, but he lacked the sureness of design of Gibbons and was prone to an excess of elaboration.

The ceilings of these Stuart rooms, which rise in a gentle cove above the cornices, are covered with frescoes representing Olympian scenes, and this was a form of decoration which was to become very popular in the decades on either side of 1700. These were the work of two Frenchmen, Laguerre and Richard, but more in demand than either of these two was the Italian, Verrio, whose handsome and elevating scenes were to be found on the walls and ceilings of many of the principal Stuart houses, including Windsor Castle. After the first quarter of the eighteenth century the fashion for murals diminished and Alexander Pope was not alone in observing them with an unappreciative eye:

> At painted ceilings we devoutly stare
> Where sprawl the saints of Verrio and Laguerre.

And yet the frescoed interiors of this period were some of the noblest produced in this country. The King's Stair at Hampton Court Palace, for example, dating from about 1690, in which the walls and ceiling are painted by Verrio with deities in an architectural framework, and Tijou created an elegant forged iron rail for the steps, strikes the proper note of splendour for a palace although the scale is not very large. It is one of Sir Christopher Wren's most successful domestic interiors, but owes more to its decoration than to its planning. Wren shares with Inigo Jones the first place in the hierarchy of English architects, but his influence on purely domestic architecture was less than is often supposed, and many country houses which were in the past vaguely attributed to Wren have been found to be by other less eminent architects.

Groombridge Place in Kent, for instance, is a charming brick house built on the moated site of an earlier building. It is just the type which is generally called 'Wrenish', but in fact is said to have been erected in 1650, many years before Wren designed his first building. Eltham Lodge, now in the outskirts of London, is another comfortable brick house which seems to show the influence of Wren but in fact was designed by Hugh May in 1663. It is considerably more sophisticated in style than Groombridge, and contains some handsome rooms with splendid plasterwork ceilings, while the finish of the whole house is of the highest quality.

The spate of country house building and alteration grew in volume as the century advanced, and the English landowner's traditional love of bricks and mortar was again able to emerge after years of suppression. An interesting house of this period is Sudbury, in Derbyshire. It was begun in the first years of the seventeenth century, but before the walls had risen more than a few feet building was abandoned, and was not continued

ight. *Section of the Great Dining Room at Wilton House, Salisbury, England, from* Vitruvius Britannicus, *Volume II. Although this book was not published until the early eighteenth century, it also included all the best buildings of the previous one. This plate of an interior from Wilton, built by Inigo Jones and Webb towards the middle of the seventeenth century, shows exactly the sort of stiff, formal grandeur of the noble house in England at this time.*

eft. The French room from Daniel Marot's Nouveau ivre d'ornements, *on the ther hand, shows a much iore relaxed and playful interpretation of the same architectural vocabulary*

until after the Restoration. Thus within what would appear a Jacobean shell are rooms decorated in the style of 1670. The white and gold drawing-room lined with carved and pedimented panels holding full-length portraits below which are swags of fruit, and with a painted ceiling – perhaps by Laguerre – set in plasterwork, is a particularly noble room of the period.

A house outstandingly rich in rooms of the 1670s is Ham House, at Richmond. Many additions to the existing building of 1610 were made by the Duchess of Lauderdale in 1673, and of the rooms she added the Cabal Room is the largest and most magnificent. It was beneath the fine plaster ceiling with its central oval wreath that the Cabal Ministry held its later meetings, but the tapestries which cover the walls date from early in the eighteenth century. However, the marble bolection moulding to the fire opening and the carved festoons surrounding the picture above it are in the true Stuart style, and the deep enriched cornice is typical of the period.

William Talman, who has already been mentioned, is connected with many country houses with varying degrees of certainty. At Dyrham Park in Gloucestershire he was working between 1698 and 1700 though whether he provided designs for the whole house is not clear. In any case the Balcony Room on the first floor, whether from Talman's drawing board or not, is a highly attractive room of the period. The walls are lined with the large panels surrounded by bolection mouldings which were in favour at the time, while the projecting chimney breast is framed with fluted pilasters which support a deep, enriched frieze. The dark colour of the panelling, with a discreet use of gilding, produces an effect of comfort and dignity without great grandeur.

In 1689 Talman was appointed Comptroller of the King's Works, and in this capacity assisted Wren in completing the interior of Hampton Court when work was re-started in 1698 after being stopped on Queen Mary's death four years earlier. The treatment of the long flights of rooms shows little variety. From the dado rail large raised panels rise to a deeply projecting wooden cornice set at about twenty-two feet above floor level; thence the ceiling rises in a plain cove well adapted to fresco painting. The fire openings are surrounded by simple marble mouldings, with, in some cases, a panel and shelf for the display of china above it. There is no indication that any of the highly elaborate

In this engraving, also from Marot, the decoration and, even more, the furniture are beginning to display the softening of rigid outline and the playfulness of form which distinguishes the flowering of the full Rococo style

designs made by Daniel Marot were carried out in the Palace, and it is improbable that they would have found much favour with the austere Dr Wren.

The years on either side of 1700 were a period of activity in country house building which has seldom been equalled, and as one reads through the pages of Celia Fiennes' *Rides through England on a Side Saddle* one gains the impression that, in the Home Counties at least, landowners of all grades were actively employed in rebuilding or embellishing their houses and in laying out gardens in the beautiful formal style that was then in favour. It was, indeed, a happy architectural period.

Palazzo Colonna, Rome

The Gran Sala: the gorgeous decoration is by Antonio del Grande and Girolamo Fontana, and the heroic ceiling paintings by Coli and Gherardi. It was completed in about 1670

Château de Maisons-Laffitte, near Paris

The ground-floor entrance hall and the first-floor landing. Cool, formal, cerebral yet wayward, this interior is completely French. Built by François Mansart and completed in 1651, the stairway is ornamented with groups of putti by Philippe de Buyster, representing the arts and sciences and with medallions by Gerard van Obstal

Hôtel Lambert, Paris

above. *Completed about 1660, this palace was designed by Le Vau. The Galerie d'Hercule, with the labours of Hercules and bronzed-plaster bas-reliefs by Van Obstal*

Ashburnham House, London

opposite. *This stair was completed in 1662, and is said to have been designed by John Webb; but whether by his hand or not it is a work of great ingenuity. Approached along a dark passage and under a low arch, it creates in a restricted area an effect of considerable grandeur*

overleaf. *The Salle des Gardes de la Reine at the Château de Versailles, France. Built to designs made by Le Vau before his death in 1670, this room with its marble-panelled walls, painted ceiling and carved woodwork forms part of the first and grandest suite in the whole palace*

Château de Vaux-le-Vicomte, near Melun, France

Opposite. The state bedroom, also known as the King's bedroom. The first owner, finance minister to Louis XIV, was accused of appropriating state funds and was committed to prison. The original furnishings were sold in 1661, and the books from the library became the basis of the Bibliothèque Nationale right. A detail of the ceiling far right. The central ceiling roundel, containing an allegorical painting of 'time carrying innocence from the sky' below. The ceiling lunette over the bed recess

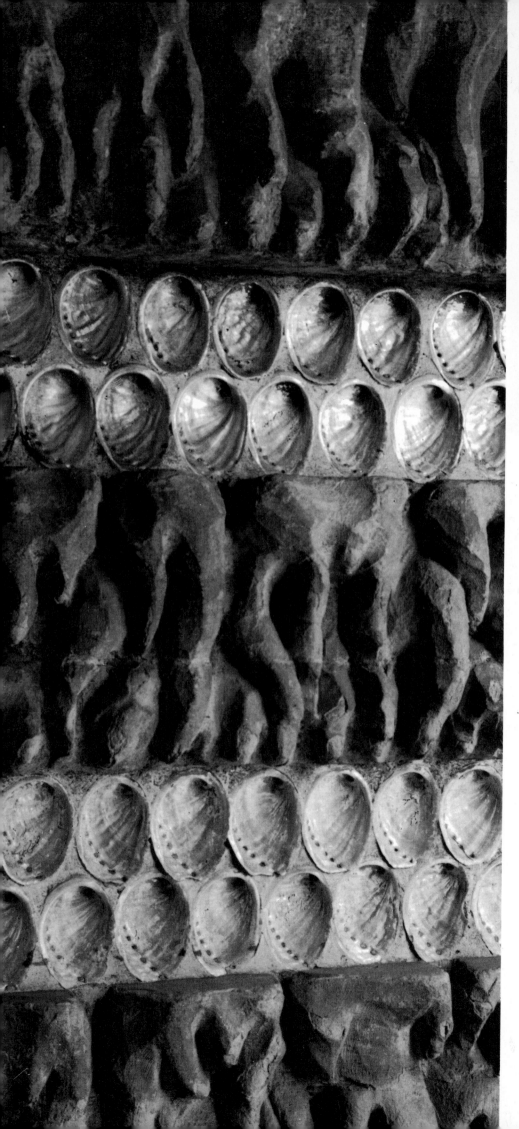

Woburn Abbey, Bedfordshire, England

opposite. This delicious and fanciful grotto dates from 1627, some twenty years before the beginning of the period under review. It has been included because it is a particularly choice example of a type of decoration which became very popular during the second half of the seventeenth century, and which in fact continued to be built until the first half of the nineteenth century. Shells, tufa, coloured gravel, and fancifully cut stones were all used to decorate this kind of room. Frequently the materials are assembled in a quasi-architectural form

Chatsworth, Derbyshire, England

The state drawing room: a detail of the fantastic carved wooden garlands round the fireplace, not by Grinling Gibbons
but by the obscure Samuel Watson. Completed to designs of William Talman round about 1690, the room
may well have been created specially to show the Mortlake tapestries, which date from some sixty years before

Hampton Court, Middlesex, England

opposite and above. *Queen Mary's bedroom. Completed about 1690, this room shows the typical unpainted panelled woodwork, silk-hung walls and general air of sombre richness of interiors of this date*

overleaf. *The staircase, Winter Palace of Prince Eugene, Vienna. The Viennese tradition of having state rooms on the upper floors made the staircase an important feature of the social parades. This staircase, completed in 1696 to designs of Johann Bernhard Fischer von Erlach, is one of the best*

opposite and above, top. *The Charles XI Gallery in the Royal Palace, Stockholm, Sweden, constructed when the palace was rebuilt after a fire in 1697, by Nicodemus Tessin the Younger. The allegorical ceiling paintings are by Jacques Fouquet. The design very closely follows French work of the same period, and may be compared with Marot's Livre d'ornements above. Door detail from the Charles XI Gallery. The doors themselves are in oak carved by Henrion to designs by Fouquet*

Burghley House, Northamptonshire, England
opposite and above. *The Heaven Room. The walls of this room were painted by Verrio in 1694*

BAROQUE AND ROCOCO 1700-50

Helena Hayward

In the first half of the eighteenth century great palaces and residences were rising throughout Europe in astonishing numbers. Not only increasing wealth but more stable conditions made this possible. The German states had at last recovered from the fears and devastations of the Thirty Years' War. Moreover, in 1683, the defeat of the Turkish hordes at the Siege of Vienna removed a menacing threat to Central Europe which had forced both noblemen and citizens to preserve their property behind medieval city walls. Before the opening of the new century, therefore, confidence was spreading and plans were being made for the erection of splendid residences outside the cramped space of walled cities and against the background of a more peaceful countryside.

If a new sense of freedom encouraged the desire to build, a vigorous and expansive optimism inspired the buildings themselves. The great Roman Baroque architects of the seventeenth century, of whom Bernini was the most widely famed, had demonstrated fresh ideals in terms of domestic architecture, and these had everywhere excited admiration. In place of austerity and reticence, an ebullient and rhythmical grandeur pervaded Roman palaces of the Baroque age. The quiet privacy of an enclosed courtyard had lost its attraction. Instead, an open forecourt revealed an animated façade, enlivened by projecting bays or wings, by the use of giant orders and sometimes by the inclusion of sculptured figures. This confident manner quickly developed in southern and northern Italy and spread to Spain and Portugal, where it was interpreted with frenzied intensity. The French version of Baroque was restrained and even Classical, but the palace of Versailles, with its disciplined magnificence, was generally acknowledged as the crowning achievement of the age.

As a result of these developments, the rulers of the numerous European states, whose interest in building was awakened in the early eighteenth century, had much to emulate, from the opulence of Italian Baroque to the formal character of Versailles. Each manner richly satisfied the political needs of the time, for the absolute power of the lesser continental despots encouraged them to regard building as a means of expressing personal omnipotence. The Prince Bishop of Würzburg, for example, impressed his subjects

and, even more important, other royal and noble rulers, by the colossal scale of his palace. But while the size and elevation of a Baroque residence were the first means of suggesting an imposing ambiance, the arrangement and decoration of the rooms themselves were vital factors. The same delight in open spaciousness which dictated the appearance of the exterior governed the interior planning. The staircase to the *piano nobile* was calculated to arouse a sense of expectation. Long vistas through the *enfilades*, or suites of rooms, leading off the central salon, on the first floor, were then revealed. Each room was not, in consequence, a separate entity but a link in a chain, carrying the eye through contrasts of colour from what appeared to be one stage setting to the next. Spatial effects were exploited also by decorative means. Frescoed walls created the illusion that the rooms themselves were no longer defined by solid structure, while a painted ceiling could transport the beholder from the confines of a mere room to the airy magic of the theatrical world. Moreover, the heroic deeds of mythical heroes which frequently formed the subject of these ceiling paintings were expressly intended to reflect the personal achievements of the patron himself. No style could have provided a better vehicle to express the needs of continental despotism and at no time had the possibilities of interior design been more daringly used.

In England, political conditions and social requirements were rather different from those elsewhere in Europe, yet here, too, a new era of peaceful prosperity encouraged noblemen and landowners to develop their country estates. Set in contrived landscapes and often containing collections of pictures and works of art, their houses represented the cultivated achievements of wealth. As an accepted convention, the Grand Tour provided an important opportunity for any young man of position both to observe the contemporary Baroque scene and to study Classical architecture. But if many English patrons were eager to have the services of Italian architects and craftsmen in the planning and decoration of their houses, the Baroque style itself found only guarded acceptance and was already losing favour in the first decades of the eighteenth century. Neither temperamentally, nor in the interests of political power, did the owners of grand country houses need to seek an essentially dramatic background for living. As a result, English Baroque rooms were treated with less regard for theatrical effect. By the 1720s, at all events, disapproval of the liberties taken by Baroque architects with the ordered system of Classical design was spreading. Palladianism was to impose a more disciplined régime in which correct proportion was vital. Bold cornices, pedimented overmantels and doorways and carefully balanced sculptural features introduced a more stable atmosphere, which in no way deprived fine interiors of dignified and sumptuous splendour. But for all its dependence on Classical example, the Palladian style was a characteristically English expression and wholly at variance with the architectural adventures which were taking place on the continent.

It was in France, just before, and shortly after, the turn of the eighteenth century that a changed approach towards the decoration of interiors was evident. Extensions and alterations to the palace of Versailles, to the Trianon and to Louis XIV's country retreat, the Château de Marly, gave the old King's architects and designers constant

opposite. The staircase at Schloss Schleissheim, near Munich, Germany, which was begun in 1704 and decorated between 1720 and 1726 by Effner, was finally completed in 1848. The interior displays a fascinating blend of Italian late Baroque and early Rococo decorative motifs

opportunities to satisfy new impulses and to evolve a fresh style. At first arabesques and ornamental fillings in panels became lighter and freer, and cornices included festoons of flowers, or even romping *putti*. Gradually, in the early years of the century, and increasingly during the *Régence*, these linear, wiry designs became more rounded and sculptural, invading the framework of the wall panelling itself to create the gracefully flowing harmony of structure and ornament characteristic of the Rococo style. By 1730, the range of decorative ornament had become more picturesque, eschewing features of Classical origin, and now uniting pastoral motifs in swirling, asymmetrical scrolls. Reflecting this escape from formality, even the planning of buildings allowed for a less orthodox arrangement of interiors and for the rooms themselves to be more varied in shape. Small salons, decorated with wit and feminine elegance, suited the growing liking of the aristocracy in France for more personal and intimate living. Parisian example was eagerly followed and, by 1750, every great room in Europe admitted the supremacy of French taste.

Baroque and Palladian Rooms

The most important room in a fine Baroque palace was the Grand Salon on the *piano nobile*, or first floor. This was the central feature of the building, approached by the grand staircase, and from which the suites of apartments on either side could be reached. Its dominating character was enhanced by imposing scale, for the ample floor space was matched by exceptional height. Unlike the surrounding rooms, the Grand Salon occupied the first floor and the mezzanine floor above. This essentially Italian arrangement of the state rooms entirely suited the aristocratic builders of the many new palaces being erected beyond the city walls of Vienna at the turn of the century. But, at first, Italian architects and artists were needed to handle such ambitious plans and unfamiliar schemes of decoration. For his Viennese *Gartenpalais*, or country residence, Prince Johann Adam von Liechtenstein, scholarly collector of paintings and works of art, who was naturally familiar with Italy, obtained the services of Domenico Martinelli. To this distinguished architect is due the superb setting of the Grand Salon. Raised above five open arcaded bays on the ground floor, it is airily poised in the centre of the garden façade. On either side it is approached by two parallel staircases, offering alternative means of reaching the first floor, and occupying the remaining bays of the same façade. Thus the room is given a spectacular position both viewed from the outside and in internal plan. Every care was taken to ensure that it created a startling impact. No hint of the rich tones and shining marble surfaces in the salon is divulged by the white and somewhat severe walls of the staircase. Nor do the small doorways leading into the room prematurely reveal the breath-taking illusion of height. Inside, the ceiling fresco seems to turn the interior into a vast open courtyard. Balconies, columns and pediments tower giddily on all sides. In the centre, Hercules is carried through windy skies, reflecting, in his triumphant apotheosis, the achievements of Prince Johann Adam. This liking for the warm, deep tones of marble, and for soaring architectural fantasies framing heroic events, was characteristic of the early years of the century. The Liechtenstein room was completed in 1708, when the artist, Andrea Pozzo, confirmed receipt of the 7,500 florins which he was paid for the work.

Since the dignity of a Grand Salon and, indeed, of the state apartments as a whole, was accentuated by the grandeur of the staircase leading to the *piano nobile*, much attention was given by Baroque architects to this important and dynamic feature. The staircase hall was virtually a room, extending sometimes through the whole height of the building. Available space at a particular site was the factor which governed the design. Where width was sufficient, the theme of the double staircase might be chosen, such as the spectacular example at Schloss Weissenstein, Pommersfelden in Germany. Here the two arms of the staircase rise in three shallow flights, following the rectangle of the hall and meeting at the entrance of the Grand Salon. Above, an arcaded gallery on the mezzanine floor allows the ceiling fresco to be seen in all its glory both from the hall below and from the staircase itself. Advice had been given on the final stages of the planning of this masterpiece by Lukas von Hildebrandt, architect to Prince Eugene of Savoy. This same architect was faced with a rather different problem a few years later, when he was working, between 1713 and 1716, on designs for the town residence of Count Daun, Imperial Viceroy of Naples. The site for this building, which the Count intended to occupy on his retirement, was exceptionally narrow, and the carriage entrance in the centre divided the two wings by a long, thin, double courtyard. This lack of width caused the main apartments to be placed on the two upper floors. The staircase, housed in one wing, rises in two long flights, one above the other, to reach the second floor. The length of each flight required ingenious planning to avoid monotony. Hildebrandt solved this by breaking each flight into three sequences of steps, divided by short landings. On the lower flight, the ceiling bay over each landing is in the form of a shallow cupola, while the corresponding wall space is broken by a niche enclosing a sculptured figure. In this way, a bare, tunnel-like effect is avoided, while the eye is attracted by what at the time was a novel motif: the stucco decoration on the ceilings, employing narrow bands of intertwining scrollwork, breaking into leaf-like fronds. Here, architect and stuccoist were inspired by designs for ornamental panels, such as those published in Germany by Paul Decker, only a few years previously. Decker himself had taken his ornamental themes from the French designer, Jean Bérain or, indirectly from him, through the Huguenot architect, Daniel Marot. Gradually, at first by means of essentially linear, decorative motifs, the influence of France was to supersede that of Italy. Hildebrandt, in fact, was translating this language of ornament into sculptural terms when he designed the most astonishing and lively feature of the staircase for Count Daun: the carved stone balustrade, mounting each flight with rollicking abandon, crowned at intervals by groups of tumbling *putti* engaged in childish struggles, and hastening the eye towards the ceiling fresco above.

The importance given to the staircase and to the state rooms in a Baroque plan did not wholly deprive the ground floor of interest. The vestibule at the base of the staircase usually communicated with a spacious room immediately beneath the Grand Salon, known as the *Sala Terrena*. This vaulted and comparatively low room, led,

BAROQUE AND ROCOCO

perhaps through an open arcade, directly into the garden, providing a cool retreat in the heat of the day. Although it served so informal a purpose, it received, nevertheless, elaborate and often quite theatrical decoration. The *Sala Terrena* at Schloss Weissenstein, Pommersfelden, was the most ambitious of the early eighteenth century in southern Germany. The palace, of which it is part, was the intensely personal expression of the will and absolute authority of Lothar Franz von Schönborn, Archbishop and Elector of Mainz and Prince Bishop of Bamberg. As Chancellor and Elector of the Holy Roman Empire, he had received, in 1711, no less than 100,000 gulden, as a reward from the Emperor Charles VI, for having successfully manoeuvred his election to the imperial throne. But even so vast a sum was insufficient to defray the costs of this spectacular building, which was not only a monument to the Prince's power, but a setting for his collection of paintings and precious objects. Porcelain, glass, ivories and bronzes claimed his interest and especially 'curiosities'. The latter covered pictures of exotic animals and natural rarities, such as shells and works of special skill, including richly veneered furniture and elaborate stucco work. In the building and planning of the interiors of his palace, he was in constant touch with his architect, Johann Dientzenhofer, and with the artists and craftsmen he employed. He corresponded at length with his cabinet-maker, Ferdinand Plitzner, and consulted with his stuccoist, Schenk, on the preparation of the stucco used for figure modelling, in order to ensure that the paste did not eventually deteriorate and turn yellow. These interests are all reflected in the decoration chosen for the *Sala Terrena*. Dientzenhofer's skilful vaulting divides the room into three sections. The pilasters carrying the dividing ribs are flanked by stucco figures representing the four Seasons and the four Elements, their poses alternating to lead the eye first into the middle and then into the outer sections of the room. The oval ceiling fresco is the central pivot, representing the various times of the day. Aurora, as morning, is drawn in her carriage across the sky, two figures with flowers and fruit symbolise the pleasures of midday, evening is a Bacchanalian feast and night a sleeping nymph. The frescoes are vividly framed in scrolling stucco work which, in the first instance, was completed in 1718. But four years later a second stuccoist, Georg Hennicke, gave the room its grotto theme, introducing stucco ornament of various colours embedded with little mirrors and small pieces of agate, crystal, mica and shells and including painted burlesque scenes, with monkeys, foxes, dragons and dolphins.

In England, early eighteenth-century Baroque interiors were arranged in the continental manner. A chain of linked apartments, in which doorways were aligned to allow a vista through each *enfilade* created a sense of unity. The state rooms, on the other hand, were usually on the ground floor, or raised only on a sunken basement. This plan lent little importance to the staircase. But it gave a vital role to the hall. Here the visitor was to receive his first impressions of the house and from this point the side apartments and the main salon, on the opposite side, were reached. Both scale and decoration had to be worthy of this central position. The cube shape was much favoured, for it allowed the hall to occupy the ground and first floor and thus to dominate the surrounding rooms. The height of the ceiling called for bold treatment. In the hall at

Moor Park, Hertfordshire, *trompe l'oeil* paintings within scrolling framework, combined with stucco figures and trophies, strive to give the great forty-foot cube a certain fluidity. The hall at Clandon Park, Surrey, completed in the late 1720s, is of the same generous dimensions. But here the Italian architect, Giacomo Leoni, imposed a more formal rhythm. The walls, regularly spaced by two tiers of engaged columns, alternating with pedimented doorways or panels, define the area with architectural clarity. Between the upper tier of columns on the inner wall, 'windows' with entablatures allow the light from the hall to penetrate into the passage running behind on the first floor level. Only the veining on the wood 'marbled' half columns and the marble surround to the over-mantels interrupt the hard brilliance of the white walls, which might almost be those of an open, sunlit courtyard. As though suspended above, like a vast canopy, by a series of delicately balanced figures, the stucco ceiling is of magnificent quality. In the corners, four Virtues are enthroned within fleshy, Italianate Baroque scrolls, divided at each side by groups of playing *putti*. In the centre, the figures of Venus and Mars are framed within a wide, circular border of interlaced strapwork. This elegant, linear ornament, if a little more crowded in treatment, is very similar to that used to decorate the stucco ceiling of the staircase in the Daun-Kinsky Palace in Vienna. It derives, in the same way, from the engraved designs of Jean Bérain, and reveals the extent of French influence, which was gradually to spread as the century advanced.

In the meantime, however, Palladian ideals were to resist the last flourishes of the Baroque style and to impose a steadying influence. In observing what was felt to be 'correct' precedents and adhering to Classical proportions, Palladian architects preferred

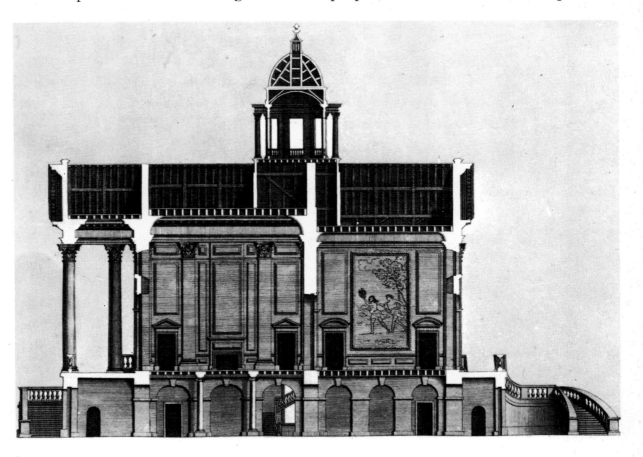

Section through Wanstead House, from Vitruvius Britannicus, *Volume I. Sober, dignified and dull, it demonstrates England's most prevalent architectural characteristics at the turn of the seventeenth and eighteenth centuries*

to place their state rooms on the first floor. This arrangement is followed at Lord Burlington's villa at Chiswick, where the *piano nobile* is reached by a double staircase on the outside of the building, leading to the entrance under the main portico. The octagonal domed salon in the centre fulfils the role of hall and salon and is surrounded by the smaller rooms. Among these, the Gallery is the most important. Here some of the pictures were hung which formed part of the collections of paintings and sculpture housed in the villa. For this was not strictly a residence, and the rooms did not have to fulfil the practical needs of living. They were planned to form a background to the collection and to be, in themselves, works of art and models of Palladian taste. The Gallery admirably achieves this purpose, for on an astonishingly small scale it is both grand and restrained. The central section, lit by a Venetian window, can be entered directly from the salon, through a pedimented doorway. Lord Burlington and William Kent conceived this as the main section of the Gallery, boldly completed by a painted and coffered ceiling, the end walls curved in the form of apses with half-domes above. But the element of surprise is not overlooked, for the apse walls are pierced with arches, revealing at each end the carved white and gilt pedimented overmantels in the sumptuous little adjoining rooms. They are observed, as it were, framed beneath the gilt half-domes of the apse walls. Adapted from a design by Palladio, the Gallery at Chiswick was not in itself an original idea, but the plan evidently pleased Lord Burlington for it was repeated both at Holkham in Norfolk and at the York Assembly Rooms.

Rococo Rooms

As an expression of the new desire for informality, Rococo interiors do not readily conform either in plan or decoration to a set pattern. Quite early in the century, in France, fine rooms composing a state suite no longer displayed the uniformity of the

These plates from Daniel Marot's Nouveau livre d'ornements *show a resolved Rococo scheme, although the details are rather crude*

Baroque system. Wood panelling, reaching to the cornice, included in the framework carved bands and leaves, intertwining perhaps with ribbons, flowers, or trophies of musical instruments. The Salon de M. le Prince in the Château de Chantilly was completed in time to receive a visit from the young King, Louis XV and the Regent in 1722. Here the decorative scheme, although in the new *Régence* manner, and of exquisite quality, reveals conservative features. The pilasters flanking the fireplace and overmantel, and the full entablature below the coved ceiling and frieze, were already beginning to be outmoded at the time. The star-like motifs in the centre of the carved panels, in which scrollwork projects to form cardinal and diagonal lines, retain also a certain conventional element. In comparison, the famous Oval Salon on the first floor of the Palais Soubise in Paris, decorated by German Boffrand for the Princesse de Soubise between 1738 and 1740, is outspokenly Rococo. The shape of the room itself, repeating the oval of the Salon du Prince on the floor below, satisfied the need for variety and harmonised with the flowing lines of the decoration. There was no longer any question of including Classical orders or an entablature. Indeed, the arches over the mirrors and doors push their way up into the coved ceiling, contriving to blur any evidence of structural features, while the frieze above, surmounted by enchanting groups of *putti*, encircles the room with rhythmical bounds. The combination of the painted spandrels by Natoire, relating the story of Psyche, with the sculptural decoration, gives this room a much greater richness than the earlier room at Chantilly possesses.

In a clearer, fresher vein is the decoration in the Grand Salon at the Château de Champs, built earlier in the century and bought by Madame de Pompadour in 1747. It was not unusual for decorative painting to illustrate romantic landscapes, exotic birds or picturesque themes, in which monkeys were shown engaged in some human activity, such as fishing or playing musical instruments. Christophe Huet had, some years earlier, painted *singeries* in the panels of the well-known salon at Chantilly, enclosing his work at that time in a scrolled, symmetrical border. At Champs, for Madame de Pompadour, he was again adding decoration to earlier panelling, but the borders with which he framed his pastoral scenes were all, by that date, frankly asymmetrical.

At each of these stages of development French Rococo interiors inspired imitators in Europe. The Elector Max Emanuel of Bavaria had exceptional knowledge of France, for he had lived in exile in the Netherlands and at St Cloud, near Paris, for some ten years, during the War of Spanish Succession. Like many of his aristocratic contemporaries, he was an enthusiastic builder with more than a superficial knowledge of architectural planning and decorative techniques. Before being driven from Bavaria by the misfortunes of war, he had already begun alterations, with the advice of Italian architects, to his palaces of Nymphenburg and Schleissheim, both near Munich. But he had experienced in France a vital period in the formation of the *Régence* style, and he returned to Bavaria in 1715 determined to introduce French elegance rather than to pursue the· grandeur of Italian Baroque. His newly appointed architect, Joseph Effner, whom he had brought to France to work under French direction on his own castle at St Cloud, was placed in charge of the work which was taken up again at his Bavarian palaces. Two Frenchmen, Charles Carbonet and Dominique Girard, were appointed to plan the Nymphenburg gardens, which included an elaborate system of waterways and fountains. Perhaps Max Emanuel's delight in water had developed in the Netherlands. At all events, his ambitions for the layout of his gardens embraced plans for garden houses – virtually miniature garden palaces. One of these was to be devoted not merely symbolically to aquatic delights, but was also to contain an actual bath some nine metres long, six metres wide and one and a half metres deep. The *Badenburg*, as this charming building was known, was designed by Effner in 1718. The entrance hall, above a sunken ground floor, is reached by an outside flight of steps. Occupying, according to Baroque precept, the height of the *piano nobile* and the mezzanine floor above, it is, in effect, also the Grand Salon, through which the smaller rooms and the bath itself are reached. Originally, the floor was of red, grey and white marble, the colours repeated in the two shell-shaped marble fountains. The ceiling fresco, destroyed in the Second World War and since repainted, also appropriately stresses the water theme, depicting nymphs and river gods fleeing before the power of the rising sun. While in conception this little garden palace is entirely Baroque, it is in the brilliant white stucco decoration of the walls, contrasting with the rich colours of floor and ceiling, that a sense of *Régence* delicacy prevails. In fact, a Frenchman, Charles Dubut, was responsible for the stucco work, in which shells and festoons combine with scrolls to fill the panels and frame the *oeil-de-boeuf* windows above. The coved frieze, with double consoles, is typically French.

If the *Badenburg* reveals Max Emanuel's admiration for France, so, more markedly, does the Grand Salon at Schleissheim, completed a few years later, in 1725. But this imposing room, vast in scale, is still a compromise between the old and the new, so characteristic of a transitional period in which a new style is evolving. Designed also by Joseph Effner, three open arches link the room with the grand staircase. The large pictures at either end depict the Siege of Vienna of 1683 and the final defeat of the Turks on that occasion. The wall panelling is divided by tall pilasters in the Baroque manner, while those in the corners, featured in perspective, are frankly in the Italian tradition. But it is in the carved wood picture frames by Adam Pichler, whom Max Emanuel had sent to Paris to be trained, and in the light and airy stucco work by Johann Baptist Zimmerman, that French *Régence* sources are evident.

The Elector Max Emanuel was so obsessed with his building plans that he spent nearly eight million florins on his palaces. In 1725 he turned his attention from his country retreats of Nymphenburg and Schleissheim to his town residence in Munich, but he died in the following year, before preparations made for a new suite of state rooms could be carried out. His successor, Karl Albrecht, the future Emperor Charles VII, continued his plans, which included, on the ground floor of an inner courtyard, the conversion of an earlier garden room into an ancestral picture gallery. Here contemporary portraits of the forbears of the House of Wittelsbach, a number of them very remote, were to be framed in the wall-panelling. While a picture gallery was a normal adjunct to a palace, the somewhat romantic idea which gave rise to this particular room was directly related to the family's imperial aspirations, which were later to be fulfilled, if only for a disastrously short time. The Residenz at Munich had been the seat of the Dukes of Bavaria since the Middle Ages, and, conscious also of his ancient lineage, Karl Albrecht reintroduced at the Bavarian Court, in 1729, the medieval Order of St George. The ceiling paintings in the new Ancestral Gallery, or *Ahnengalerie*, appropriately represent the history and introduction of the Order. But there any further reference to the past ceases, for both the carving of the panelling and the stucco work on the ceiling are in the latest fashion of the day. It seems probable that Effner originally planned the Gallery in 1726, but it was not completed before 1731. By that time, François Cuvilliés, recently appointed Court Architect, who had also studied in Paris, was in charge of the re-decoration of a number of the state apartments: a masterly designer of decorative ornament and of furniture in the 'picturesque' phase of the Rococo style, he doubtless influenced the final arrangements in the *Ahnengalerie*. In the wood carving and the stucco work, leaves and scrolls entwine fabulous animals, while *putti* scramble among flowing branches, with a total disregard for logic or symmetry, and the ceiling glitters with capricious sparkles of gold on a white ground.

Neither in the *Ahnengalerie* at Munich nor in the earlier Grand Salon at Schleissheim, however, do the ceiling paintings merge with the decorative treatment of the walls. This harmony was fully achieved in the famous Grand Salon, known as the *Kaisersaal*, at the Residenz, at Würzburg, of the Prince Bishop of Bamberg. This magnificent palace was first planned in 1720 for Johann Philip Franz von Schönborn, whose uncle built Schloss Weissenstein at Pommersfelden, with its *Sala Terrena*, already discussed. So vast an undertaking as the Würzburg Residenz took many years to complete and the interiors were not all finished before 1779. Among the state rooms, the *Kaisersaal* is the most important and the central feature of the building. In plan and elevation, and ultimately in every detail of its decoration, this room aroused the closest interest of the Prince Bishop himself and demanded detailed co-operation between architect, designers, artists and craftsmen. As

BAROQUE AND ROCOCO

Court Architect, Balthasar Neumann gave imposing height to his room, which occupies the two main floors, and is reached by a grandiose double staircase. Plans were so far executed that, by 1742, the vaults of the room were completed and shortly afterwards the marble surrounds to the doors were in place. The columns of *stucco lustro*, a material which had advantages over marble for its versatility, were designed to link the frescoes with the walls and the floor, and, through their varied tones of deep red, rose pink, blue and green, contrast with the white and pale yellow marbling of the wall-panelling behind. The work progressed slowly but, by 1749, the scaffolding was erected for the stuccoist, Antonio Bussi. In the meantime, the Prince Bishop had been considering plans for the subject to be depicted on the ceiling, prepared by two Jesuit priests, who were expert iconographers. Details for historical scenes, both for the *Kaisersaal* and for the staircase outside, were finally decided upon. It was at this stage that a disaster occurred, which was to have, paradoxically, quite exceptionally fortunate results. A travelling Italian painter, by the name of Visconti, so persuasively put forward his claims to employment that he was commissioned, in October 1749, to paint the ceiling, and stoves were duly installed so that he could work through the winter. But by March of the following year his complete incompetence was revealed. His contract was cancelled at once and, as an exposed charlatan, he was ordered to leave the city forthwith. This unexpected dilemma caused the Prince Bishop, now Karl Philip von Greiffenklau, to take an immediate and very bold step. His room was to be finest of the day so there was no alternative but to offer a tempting fee to the most famous fresco painter available. He sent his agent to Venice, with sketches of the *Kaisersaal* and iconographical plans for the ceiling, to negotiate with the great Giambattista Tiepolo. For the considerable fee of 10,000 Fl. rhn. the important commission was accepted, and Tiepolo, with his two sons and a servant, arrived at the palace on 12 December 1750, where they were housed in a suite of five rooms. Plans were immediately approved, in consultation with the stuccoist, whose own writhing cartouches and framework were ready for the gilder early in 1751. By July the Court was permitted to admire the progress of the painting, which was finally completed twelve months later.

Tiepolo's frescoes adhere faithfully to the chosen iconography. On one side of the ceiling is the marriage at Würzburg of the Emperor Barbarossa to Beatrice of Burgundy and on the other, the Parliament convened in the city by the Emperor at which he accepted the homage of the Bishopric and confirmed, in return, its privileges. In the centre panel is a mythological scene, symbolising the benefits to the city of these two historical events, for the Province of Burgundy was regained through the young bride, and Barbarossa's goodwill ensured particular rights and benefits to the city. Rising towards the centre in each of the main panels of the vaults, Tiepolo's paintings float over the vast salon, creating an atmosphere of flickering sunlight and airy spaciousness. His characters are shown in Renaissance costume, indicating that the scenes were historical and not contemporary, but his imaginary portrait of Beatrice of Burgundy, far from showing her as the very young girl which she was, present a beautiful and mature Venetian blonde. In fact, the silver sparkle of Venice crowns this sumptuous room, which is among the grandest conceptions of the Rococo style.

Long section of the gallery of Mr Wyndham at Hammersmith. By comparing this plate with the section through Wanstead House, one can see how English interior design was developing

While Italian artists and craftsmen were eagerly employed throughout Europe in the decoration of Rococo interiors, those working in their own native cities were often required to cater for more traditional, late Baroque taste. In Rome, very naturally, the Classical manner represented the official style, but some members of the aristocracy were prepared to be less orthodox in their taste. The wing added to the Palazzo Doria by Gabriele Valvassori between 1731 and 1734, for example, has an animated Rococo façade, and contains the magnificent Gallery, in which the liveliness of the gilt panelling is matched by the grandiloquence of the console tables.

Two of the great centres of what, at the time, was essentially modern taste were Piedmont, in the north, and Naples, in the south. At Turin, capital of Piedmont, the royal palace contains magnificent apartments redecorated for Carlo Emmanuele III of Savoy and his queen, to the designs of the Court Architect, Filippo Juvarra. The little salon on the *piano nobile*, entirely lined with panels of Chinese lacquer, obtained for the purpose by Juvarra in Rome, is of a delicacy and discipline characteristic of the architect. Completed about 1735, the carving of the gilt frames, in which the lacquer panels are set, and of the overdoors and door panels, is in a restrained and coherent Rococo style. The brilliance of the colours, on the other hand, consisting of a rich red with black and gold, contrasting with the brown and orange tones of the parquetry floor, is quite unexpected. The Queen's Dressing Room in the palace, forming part of her suite of private apartments on the first floor, was also sumptuously decorated in these years. Here, mirrors mounted in the wall-panelling reflect the flowing lines and gay surfaces of the marquetry furniture made specially for the room by the Court cabinet-maker, Pietro Piffetti. Both these little rooms, typical of the age in their intimate scale and elegance, exhibit also a Rococo delight in the use of unusual or exotic material to form decorative panelling. Both mirrors and panels of Oriental lacquer had long been admired. But porcelain, still comparatively new and rare as a European product, was to inspire a new fashion. The factory at Capodimonte earned wide renown by providing, in the late 1750s, some three thousand porcelain plaques needed in order entirely to line a little salon in the royal villa at Portici, near Naples. Of varying shapes, the white plaques were made to fit together, while porcelain mouldings, figures of Chinamen and festoons of flowers, were modelled and applied to cover the joins. This wonderfully skilful and colourful room gleams with the brilliance of white glaze, echoed in the white and gold ceiling above. The mood of fantasy is enhanced by the porcelain chandelier, suspended from the ceiling and held in a monkey's paw.

BAROQUE AND ROCOCO

While these extravagant decorative schemes were planned at the fashionable centres of Rococo taste, the aristocrats of Genoa, many of them in close contact with Paris, were both sufficiently wealthy and eager to adopt the modern trends. The Carrega family, for example, purchased in the eighteenth century a splendid late Renaissance Genoese palace, originally designed for a certain Tobia Pallavicini. A storey was added to increase its size and, in 1744, the re-decoration included Lorenzo de Ferrari's *Galleria Dorata*, or Golden Gallery, so named on account of the incredible richness of the gilt panelling and stucco work. The painted ceiling and overdoors, recounting the adventures of Aeneas, are rather sombre in tone, while the unrelieved gilding of the panelling adds an impression of ponderous magnificence. The most astonishing feature of the room is the doors, in which carved and gilt leaves and scrolls surrounding exotic winged creatures, rising improbably from Classical stools, are mounted on a background of mirror panels. With French Rococo such decorative treatment would have been unthinkable, and yet the Genoese version is quite individual and has an almost gross energy which recalls the powerful seventeenth-century days of this essentially Baroque city.

English houses altered little in internal plans as the eighteenth century advanced. But towards 1740, a greater degree of informality in social conduct and a growing delight in nature were reflected both in the scale of rooms and in their decoration. The Great Hall became less dominant and state rooms more intimate in size and arrangement. This new flexibility accorded with continental practice. On the other hand, the decorative style adopted in these English rooms was strangely inconsistent and presented a curious contrast with the various aspects of European Rococo. Rooms decorated with such extravagant brilliance as the Queen's Dressing Room in the royal palace in Turin or with so disciplined a sense of luxury as the Salon de la Princesse at the Palais Soubise in Paris were too sophisticated for English tastes. English architects, setting up their practices in the 1730s, had been trained in the Palladian tradition, but they were torn between two conflicting worlds. In the decorative treatment of interiors they might either observe Classical rules of proportion and draw their motifs from 'correct' sources, or succumb to the modern fashion set by French ornamental designers and introduce Rococo features. Isaac Ware proposed a solution to this predicament in his *Complete Body of Architecture* (1756). In his view, a successful architect had to learn to compromise, for 'unless he can conform himself to fancy, as well as work with judgment, he will do little in an age like this'. Ware, of course, was writing after the middle of the century, when it would have been useless to deny the appeal of Rococo. By then the style represented a respectable deviation from the Classical norm. But the need to compromise was apparent by the 1730s, when Palladian taste was seriously challenged by a group of young artists centred on the St Martin's Lane Academy, founded by William Hogarth in 1735. Originally set up as a school for figure drawing, this Academy soon widened its activities and attracted vigorous young artists, architects, sculptors and designers, ready to exploit the new freedom of the Rococo style, and among whom were a number of Frenchmen. It was in this stimulating international atmosphere that the youthful James Paine had studied drawing. Here, his interest in French example first evolved, although, as a newly practising architect, he had

Section of Sir Robert Ladbrook's House at Foots Gray, from Volume VI of Vitruvius Britannicus

adopted the established Burlingtonian style. The result of these interests was revealed in his first commission at Nostell Priory, Yorkshire, undertaken in 1733. With his patron, Sir Rowland Winn, Paine designed a strictly Palladian plan and elevation. The main suite of apartments on the *piano nobile*, however, decorated about 1740, only half-heartedly retained a semblance of these principles. But the compromise did not end with the contrasting formality of the exterior and more lenient character of the interior. The Rococo stucco decoration on walls and ceilings was somewhat inconsistently imposed, as it were, upon a Palladian framework. The dining-room at Nostell Priory illustrates this early phase of English Rococo, strangely contradictory and yet confidently elegant. The room lies on the garden façade, between what was originally described as the 'common sitting room', in the south-west corner of the building, and the salon in the centre, with a vista through to the library at the other end of the suite. The overmantel is in the tradition of William Kent and yet it is enlivened by floral festoons and scrolls and triumphantly dominated by a basket of jostling flowers on the central bracket, overflowing on to the curving arms of the pediment itself. The Palladian character of the architectural frames on the end walls is also discreetly weakened by the inclusion of a bird, with outstretched wings, taking flight from a scrolled cartouche within the pediment, and the presence of curving leaves wreathing the uprights. The stucco relief on the ceiling is contained within a sober, oval frame, but the outer border is lightly entwined with vine leaves, an appropriate motif for a dining room, and engagingly suggestive of Rococo designs of the next decade. But there is no aggressive expression of asymmetrical ornament and even the stucco cartouches, which appear in the corners of the ceiling and at the central points at each side, are contained within formal borders. Similar compromises were familiar at the time and a variation occurs in the decoration of the dining-room at Kirtlington Park, Oxfordshire, now in the Metropolitan Museum, New York. This room was completed rather later than that at Nostell Priory and although the Rococo scrollwork is bolder, it is,

BAROQUE AND ROCOCO

nevertheless, contained, on the ceiling, within a formal framework.

An example of a highly original early Rococo room survives at Honington Hall, Warwickshire. Here an octagonal salon was added to the existing house in about 1745 and the disturbance which this caused to the unity of the façade in no way offended the new liberal taste. The domed, octagonal form echoes that of Lord Burlington's salon at Chiswick House and of James Gibb's Octagon at Orleans House, Twickenham. At first sight, the ceiling of the Honington room seems wholly Palladian in character, but a closer look reveals bands of Rococo stucco work dividing each section of the Octagon. In the decoration of the walls the most unexpected features are the rich and rather heavy Rococo stucco drops at the angles, matching, in a slightly ponderous manner, the plaster mirror frames. As a material capable of quick manipulation, it is not difficult to see how great was the advantage of using stucco rather than wood. The stuccoists themselves moved quickly from one job to another, while records establishing their personal achievements are few. The work in the salon at Honington, however, suggests an Italian hand, for although the theme is often outspokenly Rococo, the execution betrays the natural Italian tendency to cling to the spirit of their native Baroque.

While the treatment of interiors in English country houses gradually admitted Rococo, the style could also be accepted even in academic circles. The magnificent Library at Christchurch College, Oxford, is a long rectangular room, lined with bookcases of traditional architectural design. At intervals along the walls above and on the coved ceiling are symmetrical stucco cartouches in white, on a delicately coloured ground. This arrangement stresses the decorative nature of Rococo as a style and by the 1750s its appeal became more insistent. It was quite natural, in consequence, for existing rooms in houses of earlier date, even though they were originally Baroque conceptions, to be re-designed in the new manner. The Great Hall at Ragley, Warwickshire, for example, was given a more fashionable appearance very shortly after the middle of the century. The result is, of course, a compromise. A splendid stucco ceiling, in which the central relief is surrounded surrounded by foaming white scrolls, now crowns this lofty hall, of which the bold proportions recall those of Clandon Park, Surrey. Where Clandon, however, retains undisturbed its stately clarity, the walls at Ragley have also been enlivened by the addition of stucco trophies, festoons and cartouches. The use of these features is typically English. But in their execution and design the sense of compromise is doubly stressed, for the Italian stuccoist, lending his work a certain characteristic weight, took his cue, inevitably, from France. This room illustrates, in fact, the international element in the spread of fashion. At the same time, in combining a Baroque plan with Rococo decoration, it brings together the opposing ideals of grandeur and informality – qualities which had distinguished so many great rooms in Europe in the first half of the eighteenth century.

Honington Hall, Warwickshire, England

opposite. *The Octagon Salon. This room was added to the existing house in about 1745, to a design from an unknown hand. Whilst at first sight the room appears to be Palladian, the decorative details are Rococo*

Thurn und Taxis Residenz, Regensburg, Germany

The ballroom, built between 1730 and 1740 to designs of Robert de Cotte, Hauberat and Paul Egell. The whole interior was transferred to Regensburg from the family castle in Frankfurt in 1895. The furniture dates from the early nineteenth century

Prince Eugene's Winter Palace, Vienna

right. The Gold Salon, designed in 1704. All the visible woodwork is covered in gold leaf and arabesque paintings, and the effect is one of fantastic richness

Palazzo Doria, Rome

opposite. The Gallery, built by Gabriele Valvassori in 1731–4. Rococo never achieved the liveliness in Italy that it did in France and Germany; all the decoration is painted

'Sans Souci', Potsdam, Germany

The oval cupola room, which was completed by Georg Wenzeslaus von Knobelsdorff for Frederick the Great in 1749, to the King's designs. This sumptuous room was used as an informal dining room

Badenburg, Nymphenburg, near Munich, Germany

opposite and right. *This pavilion was designed by Effner and built between 1718 and 1721 as a bath house for the Elector Max Emanuel in the grounds of his summer palace. The Grand Salon (opposite page), has elaborate stucco ornaments by Charles Dubut, a French sculptor, and a ceiling originally painted by Amigoni. The bath (right), in the basement, is tiled in blue and white delft whilst the upper walls have a black and white stucco–marble treatment*

right and overleaf. *Salon de M. le Prince, Château de Chantilly, near Paris, France. This room, completed in 1722, is one of the most beautiful of its kind in existence. The quality of the workmanship in the carved panelling and the white and gold colouring combine to give it great charm*

The Governor's Palace, Williamsburg, Virginia, USA

The Supper Room. Originally built for Governor Spotswood in about 1730, the palace was burnt down in 1781; in 1928 it was reconstructed and the beautiful interior furnished with antiques, glass, silver and fabrics of the period. The lovely pale blue Chinese wallpaper of the Supper Room came from a house in Mayfair, London, which was being demolished at the time

Royal Palace, Madrid

right, opposite and overleaf.
*The Gasparini Salon.
Although decorated by Matias
de Gasparini in 1765–70,
this room combines elements
of the wildest Rococo with an
unexpected rigidity in the
cornice and door-openings.
The walls are hung with
green and yellow silk, and the
set of chairs is carved in
tulipwood. The chandelier
and other pieces of furniture
are of a much later date*

Palais Soubise, Paris
This lovely room, the Salon Ovale, was decorated by Germain Boffrand for the Princesse de Soubise between 1738 and 1740. The oval form, the flowing lines and the unified treatment of ceiling and walls combine to produce practically every special effect associated with full Rococo

Chiswick House, Middlesex, England

The Gallery. This apartment runs the length of one side of the house. It was completed in 1729 for Lord Burlington to the designs of his architect William Kent, and was intended solely as a setting for parties and concerts and to house pictures and works of art

Munich Residenz, Germany

The Ahnengalerie. Completed in about
1731 under the direction of François
Cuvilliés, the court architect of the time,
this great gallery was built for Duke Karl
Albrecht of Bavaria, to display portraits
of his ancestors. The portraits were however considered secondary to the brilliant
scheme of decoration which runs along the
length of the room, and which has
recently been restored

Würzburg Residenz, Germany

The Kaisersaal. This room is one of the grandest Rococo conceptions, and demonstrates the complete fusion of all decorative elements, found only in great artistic productions. The decoration of this room went on for many years, and although Balthasar Neumann had the structure ready by 1742, Giambattista Tiepolo did not begin work on the famous ceiling until 1750. right and far right. Details of the figures and decoration on the walls

Schloss Schleissheim, near Munich, Germany

opposite and below. *The Kaisersaal. This room was completed in 1725 to designs by Joseph Effner, and shows in its decorative treatment an intriguing combination of old and new elements of the period*

NEO-CLASSICAL 1750-90

Terence Davis

It would be difficult to find a country in the world without its neo-classical buildings and these buildings might date from Palladio's villas of the sixteenth century to the present day: St Peter's, Rome; Melk; the Louvre; Versailles; Bath; the White House; Williamsburg – to cite famous instances – are buildings or groups of buildings that owe their appearance to elements of earlier Classical design and their architects used their knowledge and belief in these to produce buildings suited to contemporary needs and tastes.

But Neo-classicism with a capital 'N' denotes a specific time in architectural history when Europe was dedicated to a proper understanding of ancient Classical design and a serious attempt to prove that all previous uses of Classical elements had been wrongly based and that, above all, the undisciplined and frivolous abandon of Baroque and Rococo were beneath contempt. This desire to recapture the basic qualities found in ancient Greek and Roman buildings was founded on new archaeological discoveries and a more serious study of the principles involved in the use of Classical elements. Each element, whether decorative or not, had to serve a rational purpose and some of the strictest theorists of the movement even wished for decoration of any sort to be omitted, in the search for purity and truth. This was, needless to say, the extremists' dream and in fact Neo-classical decoration was to create its own excesses and contradictions as the style developed during the last half of the eighteenth century. But the movement was strong enough to have great influence on building and decoration for some fifty years and much longer, if one takes into account the time-lag created by geographical circumstances.

In their different ways, French, English and, to a lesser extent, Italian architects evolved their own Neo-classical styles which spread, via tenuous and various influences, to Spain, Portugal, America and Russia. But it was England and France who were the leaders; they influenced each other and in turn influenced Italy – the source of their newly-gained knowledge of archaeology and architecture. There were, however, personal battles of style to be fought and distillations of principles to be accepted owing to personal prejudices and the inevitability of certain architects to produce individual versions of *any* style. The Frenchman Abbé Laugier advocated that Grecian standards were the ones to

opposite. The tea room, Palace of Queluz, near Lisbon, Portugal. Begun in 1758, this little summer palace contains whole suites of rooms in the Rococo style with great use made of native tiles. This room is rather more severe than most, and may be compared with the Gold Salon at Prince Eugene's Winter Palace in Vienna, built some fifty years earlier

NEO-CLASSICAL

follow, which angered G. B. Piranesi who, in several important volumes of engravings, extolled the virtues of Imperial Roman architecture; Robert Adam's dazzling expertise owed most to Roman origins and little to Greek; others were loyal to Greek ideals.

But we must look more closely into the complex of the battle of styles, a subject lucidly explored by Mr James Lees-Milne in his *Age of Adam*, before we proceed to consider its results, for it is the people who preceded Adam and his contemporaries who instigated and led the controversy between Greek and Roman design.

Piranesi (1720–78) remained a diehard 'Roman' (though later he modified his views somewhat) but a formidable number of champions of Greek ideals were emerging in direct opposition to his published pronouncements – ideals that would cause a dilemma in Neo-classical thought and would make certain appearances in buildings throughout the civilised world during the latter half of the eighteenth century and again in a final burst of neo-Greek enthusiasm at the beginning of the nineteenth. Piranesi's most powerful 'Greek' rival was the Abbé Winckelmann, an eccentric German of humble origin who, after years of strenuous toil, elevated himself into the undisputed position of chief arbiter of architectural learning in Rome. With his close friend Raphael Mengs and at first under the protection of Cardinal Passionei, he appeared to sift cultured foreign visitors according to their Greek or Roman inclinations; thus James 'Athenian' Stuart became a firm favourite but Robert Adam, although he used Greek ornament and appreciated the merits of both Greek and Roman principles, came under the spell of Piranesi. In 1775 Winckelmann published his laborious *Thoughts upon the Imitation of Greek Works of Art in Painting and Sculpture* which established the author as the first serious theorist to assess the value of the artistic achievements of ancient civilisations. After the publication of his *Observations upon the Architecture of the Ancients* (1760) and his *History of Ancient Art* of 1763, his reputation as the most distinguished art-historian of his day was firmly established. The latter was translated into English and forms part of his influence on the development of Classical design – an influence that halted the excess of Rococo in France, that spread the appreciation of ancient architecture, and paved the way for a clearer basis on which his followers could found the ideals of Neo-classicism. Winckelmann's direct influence on architecture and design was, however, not immediate and those in Europe who belonged to the Greek cause were not strong enough personalities to establish a Greek revival of any importance.

France In 1750 France, the cradle of the Neo-classical theorists, decoration was ruled by Rococo. Unlike German or Italian Rococo it took the basic form of small-scale decoration for panelling, as we can see in Verberckt's Petit Trianon. The style was free and irrational and, in the hands of indifferent designers, often merely achieved licence and turgidity. But now various forces were working which intended to kill this lack of scholarship and disregard of the true purpose of Classical ornament and it is at this moment that we see the birth of Neo-classical building. Apart from the *avant garde* architects and designers of the period there were writers, teachers and professional and amateur theorists at work, the most prominent being Cochin, Blondel and Laugier, the latter exercising profound influence on architects but all three forming the first of two streams of influence. Even before this the Abbé de Cordemoy had condemned in his *Nouveau Traité* of 1706 the use of ornament for its own sake and the careless use of Classical detail. Laugier echoed these sentiments in 1753 in his *Essai sur l'Architecture* and so began the first carefully-considered Classical French interiors although, as we have noted, each designer of merit had his own way of interpreting the ideals and few, if any, obeyed the strict rules laid down by de Cordemoy.

The second stream of influence was the new archaeological discoveries of the first half of the century. The Greek temples at Athens and Paestum and the Roman ruins at Herculaneum and Pompeii were the sources of element and ornament. Greek buildings and Wincklemann's teaching inspired a new taste for simplicity and the Roman ruins were found to contain a richness of decoration very different from their grandiose 'official' exteriors. Archeologists went further afield and culled decorative motifs from Egypt and Syria to add to the designers' vocabulary. It was the beginning of a new eclecticism which at worst would mean the use of ornaments of various cultures for the sake of novelty and at best, in the hands of talented innovators, could be used in the formation of a new style. Those patrons who could afford to indulge in this new vocabulary were likely to have some appreciation of the antique and there was a rising group of architects ready to put things in proper perspective and to fight the ignorance and excesses of their predecessors.

The two most successful French Neo-classical architects were Jacques-Germain Soufflot (1713–80) and Claude-Nicolas Ledoux (1736–1806); the former was the greater, the latter the more original. Soufflot had studied at first hand for seven years in Rome and upon his return to France was taken up by Madame de Pompadour and appointed mentor to her brother, M. de Marigny, who was later to become *Surintendant des Bâtiments*. Soufflot was championed and profoundly influenced by the strict Laugier and his buildings showed the fashionable veneration for antiquity and sometimes bordered on dullness.

Ledoux, in sharp contrast, whilst also a firm advocate of the Orders, was more inventive and never dull. Like his great Classicist contemporary, Gabriel, he did not study in Italy, and relied on Piranesi's dramatic engravings as a source of decorative detail. His Hôtel de Montmorency of 1770 displayed his skill and originality in planning rooms of oval and circular shape – an idea developed by Adam and used later by Soane, Nash and others in the English school. A year later he designed the Pavillon de Louveciennes for Madame du Barry and here we see interior decorations in true French Neo-classical style with no excesses, no cluttered panels and with pilasters and Classical reliefs used sparingly and to much effect. The celebrated Hôtel Thélusson of 1782 (but completed some years later) is another Paris house of great importance and again shows Ledoux's genius for manipulating shapes and applying Roman decoration with enlightened discretion. Here we also see influence in reverse, for the house is approached by an English-style garden, elements of which were also to be dotted about the gardens of Versailles, thus contrasting Classical austerity with Romantic surroundings. Ledoux was to develop this cult for the Romantic and Picturesque in many ways although it was to differ in several respects from the English version. Soon English-style gardens were to spread over northern Europe and later, less appropriately, to Italy.

NEO-CLASSICAL

Lesser talents, too, made their mark with varying degrees of success throughout this period and with all their divergences they were committed to the basic aim to treat Classical design seriously, however differently the results turned out in various hands.

During their Neo-classical phase French rooms never lost their all-over sense of unity and there is seldom an exaggeration of particular elements either by articulation in plane or in surface treatment. Vaulted ceilings are compartmented to reflect pilasters and panelling of walls and rarely used as an opportunity to display an autonomous design as did Adam and American designers. The French desire for unity reaches the ultimate in non-classical terms with trellis-covered walls and ceilings painted to resemble the sky.

The beginning of French Neo-classicism saw a return to the *Grande Manière* and from 1750 *Le Style Louis XIV* was formulated. This return to grandeur was coupled with a growing taste for small intimate rooms; little secret boudoirs and closets providing the ideal climate for sensuous hedonism; doors were concealed in panelling behind which amorous escapades might be played out. But, for all its richness, the decoration of these rooms was more disciplined than hitherto and paid more tributes to the archaeological ideal. Classical elements were used with more logic and, depending on their importance and size, either panelled or decorated with pilasters; however elaborate and sumptuous the effect, the details 'made sense'. The extreme idea that all decoration should be omitted was, of course, completely ignored; but a rational use of ornament had resulted from stricter theories. This comparative astringency contrasted strongly with earlier French rooms where the over-use of small panels crammed with minuscule grotesques and arabesques and multiplication of small mouldings and motifs often produced a negative effect and contrasts, too, with English and some Italian decoration of the period. After about 1775 motifs such as the Greek key pattern and the wave motif appear more frequently in duty to Greek archaeology, first being applied to furniture and then spreading to wall surfaces and fabrics. Although designers professed (and probably tried) to use the Greek Orders in their original form this, in fact, was rarely done; the Greek happened to supply the demand for simplicity but, in detail, a Doric column or pilaster often implied a version of Tuscan, whilst Ionic sometimes implied a Roman Doric Order perhaps without fluting and freely adapted to suit the room. A little later motifs became increasingly shallow and, as in Marie Antoinette's suite of rooms at Versailles, smaller in scale and more refined. Although the period did not see a return to elaborate over-all decoration for the sake of elaboration alone, large rooms, more suited to grand treatment, were covered with profusions of delicate decorations. And, against the general flow of Neo-classicism, others, notably Veberckt and Antoine Rousseau, still purveyed Rococo interiors twenty years after Laugier, Soufflot and Ledoux had laid down the Neo-classicists' law.

A fashion that we think of as essentially French was the use of vegetation and other natural forms in decoration. Palms, plants and flowers of every description were entwined in trellis, allowing views of picturesque countryside, and gave boudoirs an impression of eternal summer, echoing the Picturesque movement that emanated from England. The English concentrated on the relationship of buildings to their surroundings; the French brought the picturesque scenes indoors. Humble tackle such as rakes, baskets and spades

evoked a vision of the ideal countryside and the unsophisticated sheep and cattle were woven into scenes and trophies to conjure up the simple pleasures of rustic life. Artists working in this idiom were Boucher, Lalande, Cauvet, Ranson, J-B. Huet, and Peyrotte.

Another by-way in decoration was the cult of the Oriental, although this did not flourish as well in France as it did in England and Italy. Nevertheless the period embraced an interest in the exotic, the results being mainly confined to Chinese garden kiosks and 'Turkish' boudoirs. Oriental scenes and other exotic decorations would be used in rooms but usually within the limits of a Classical setting of panels and pilasters.

French Neo-classicism was therefore a strong force in spite of its absconders, influencing England and being influenced by her in return and both, in their different ways, preaching the ideals for almost the same length of time. Several of the leaders of the movement had travelled from Paris, London and Madrid to study antiquities in Rome between the 1730s and the 1760s and had returned with a strong determination to adapt and use their knowledge with conviction. This they did with utterly different results: Soufflot's sombreness, Adam's sparkle and the Spanish Villanueva's scholarship. England was a little later than France, Spain later still.

Italy

Italy, on the other hand, whilst remaining the Mecca and inspiration, never became a stronghold of the Neo-classical style. The buildings that were designed in the last half of the century were often Neo-classical but the interiors nearly always retained the characteristics of former centuries; anything that succeeded the masterpieces of the Renaissance or, indeed, the Palladian villas, was bound to seem shadowy. There were other reasons, too, why Italian Neo-classicism was weak: although Italy produced Palladio – the first great architect – other influences such as Rococo came to Italy later than to France and England; she had not yet had her fill of the frivolous curls and twirls of this style of decoration by the time others had got the principles of Neo-classicism firmly established. One will therefore often see rooms of Rococo and Neo-classical flavour side by side in houses built earlier than either style. It is also to be noted that the Italians interested in the Neo-classical movement were not architects but theorists and, as is often the case, the theorists themselves were at loggerheads. Friar Lodoli (1690–1761), a Venetian priest whose *Elementi d'architettura lodoliana* sets out his functional Neo-classicism, was in earnest opposition to his contemporary Milizia who felt that the legacy of antiquity was exhausted. Piranesi was a figure of importance and although trained as an architect he seldom practised it. But his engravings inspired the Neo-classicists to appreciate antiquity and it was with his *Della magnificenza ed architettura de' Romani* (1761) that he attempted to wean the French Neo-classicists away from Greek antiquities. His powerful etchings, to become Ledoux's and Adam's most valuable references, evoked an effect of extreme grandeur and provided sources of ornament for many architects but there is little evidence that they had much influence on Italian architecture of the time. His imaginative designs in *Parere su l'architettura* (1765) were sometimes built up of many unrelated elements thrown together without much thought for archaeological accuracy or topographical correctness; they show a certain sense of disintegration, each element being treated as something isolated, of equal claim to importance and often out of scale. But their dramatic and magnetic qualities are unparalleled and the French and English exponents lost no time in borrowing the ornaments and elements they needed to build up their own vocabularies.

In some Italian Neo-classical work can be seen Piranesi's lack of regard for related ornament and to show how far England had leapt ahead in her development of authoritative architectural style, Count Algarotti left Italy to visit England in the 1730s to preach Ludoli's faith in simple design: 'In architecture only that shall show that has a definite function and which derives from the strictest necessity . . .'; he found, however, that Lord Burlington had already assimilated the faith he had come to preach and for the first time in history we see English architects exercising influence on Italian design and thought. The Palazzo Pisani de Lazzara by Selva (1783) shows that this influence of chaste Classicism persisted late into the century and the Palazzo Braschi, Rome, with its domed circular salon, echoes Adam at Kedleston and his project for Syon. The salon reminds us of Adam's Pompeian-Etruscan manner of decoration; its predominantly light colour scheme with darker painted figures and motifs and the tabernacle-like ornaments of the dome linked by garlands show an Italian Neo-classical room at the height of its brief flowering.

But it was not until Palazzo Braschi was built (from 1791) that we can say that a Neo-classical style really existed in Italy. Until then Rococo was still running its late course – the curling tendrils of the style being plastered on otherwise Classical compositions; or one

would find a building lacking all ornament but conveying a Rococo feeling such as Vanvitelli's Villa Campolieto of 1760. This feeling was given by a certain plasticity, with details applied merely for textural interest rather than ornament – the exact opposite of what Neo-classicism stood for and against which Milizia fought. Utterly irresponsible, the style favoured rooms containing delicate stuccoed or painted tendrils forming frames for rustic or exotic frescoed scenes often flowing onto the vaulted ceilings as at Villa Agnelli (1760–70). At this time also *trompe l'oeil* was used almost to the limit and the smooth plaster walls and vaults of *sala d'onore* at the Villa detta degli Amoretti were riotous and covered with colourful architectural frescoes. Here the scheme is grey-blue and yellow with painted designs that suggest elaborate pilasters, panel recesses and windows, all of stage-set unreality. The traditional passion for painted decorations of this nature on ceilings and walls lasted late into the century, as can be seen at the Palazzo Reale at Caserta started by Vanvitelli (1760–73), where the sumptuous palace first commissioned by Carlos III in 1751 contains decorations that range in style from frankly French excesses, through magnificent Baroque expression to delicately painted ceilings executed in 1790, long after Vanvitelli had vanished from the scene. Only the restrained exterior reminds us that Neo-classicism touched the Palazzo Reale; the interior fits our dates but scarcely fits the ideals being forged by the French and English architects of the time.

With long-lasting Rococo went a passion for *Chinoiserie* – often as good and sometimes more authentic than anything outside English decoration in that vein. Houses contained painted wallpaper of Chinese and other exotic scenes set in Rococo swirls and G.B. Tiepolo contributed his own strictly 'Western-Chinese' scenes which were flanked by frescoed niches and columns in a neo-Gothic room of extravagant brilliance at Villa Valmarana, Vicenza, of the 1750s; but this is an isolated decoration phenomenon as neo-

Gothic does not appear again until the nineteenth century. *Chinoiserie* decorations continued, however, until the 1770s, the most elaborate being the celebrated porcelain room at Capodimonte, Naples, of 1757.

Several other palaces and villas possess Neo-classical elements but certainly what there was of a real movement started tentatively without a catharsis and was mainly French in origin. At Piedmont we find flat pilasters supporting a straight entablature, coffered or panelled vaults, and panels filled with arabesques and grotesques – but all less cluttered than their early French originals; the Classical ornaments are allowed to 'breathe' and to be appreciated for their own sakes, with a complete absence of anything remotely Rococo.

The spread of Neo-classicism to Spain and Portugal was even less obvious but Juan de Villanueva (1739–1811), a late-comer to the Roman scene and previously schooled in the Baroque, carried back to Madrid a strong belief in the movement and reacted against the flamboyance of his predecessor, Churriguera – a hard fight in the teeth of traditional Spanish Baroque and Rococo extravagances. But he made his mark and the simplicity of the Prado, inside and out, testifies to his assimilation of the style and all that it meant. Portugal, too, felt the influence of the style at Oporto where John Carr of York's work of 1769 can be seen and in the rebuilding of Lisbon after the earthquake of 1775 when the celebrated Terreiro do Paco was a tribute to the French interpretation of Neo-classicism. Other examples of the revolt against Baroque were scattered over Portugal after 1750 but many important rooms, though Neo-classical in date, are Baroque in effect.

England

England had seen the first signs of scholarly Classicism in the earlier part of the century when Burlington and Kent were building according to Palladio's translation of antiquities. As we have seen, Burlington had surprised Algarotti with his expertise and was to establish Palladianism firmly for many years until it petered out against the competition of the Picturesque. But between Palladianism and the Picturesque came Neo-classicism which was England's attempt to improve her previous knowledge of Classical architecture.

Section through the main
rooms of the Hôtel Thélusson,
Paris, built by C.N.
Ledoux in 1782. The Neo-
classical style in France at this
date was very architectural, as
can be seen in these interiors
by an architect better known
for his theories than his
buildings

Palladio was not good enough; original antiquities must be explored at first hand and properly understood. By the middle of the century, the *Grand Tour* was no novelty, but Adam was the first professional British architect to visit Italy (1754–8) to study not Palladio but Imperial Roman architecture.

The word 'Adam' or 'Adams' has been much abused and misunderstood. Either word has often been applied loosely to anything designed by Robert's father William (1689–1748), a distinguished Scottish architect, his partner-brother James or himself; worse, 'Adam-style' has confused the issue even more and is today applied to almost every modern chimney-piece or decoration scheme bearing the remotest relationship to designs by the hand of the master, Robert. His *immediate* influence, however, was of a different order and we see versions of his doorways and other ornamentation used in thousands of large and small terrace houses many years after his death and, unlike the decorative parodies of today, were hardly ever wrongly used or so debased as to be meaningless.

In Rome Robert Adam was guided by Charles-Louis Clérisseau (1721–1820), a French architect of small talent but with great ability to influence his pupils and followers (who included William Chambers and Thomas Jefferson) in the Neo-classical cause. Adam returned from Italy with a large vocabulary of antique ornament which he was to adapt and use with a brilliance unknown before or since his time. His early commissions consisted of additions and remodellings of existing houses but he soon established his own completely individual style that included not only the design of a whole house but its entire contents – decorations, furniture and furnishings down to the smallest key escutcheon. Before long this ruthlessly ambitious Scot had captured more work than any architect in England and only James Wyatt (1746–1813) could be said to offer any serious competition to him. Although his decorations were opulent and richly designed they were never ostentatious, never pretentious; with the greatest skill he manipulated ornament and colour, spaces and shapes into interiors of matchless elegance. Contrived with an aim to add a new dimension to room shapes his plans, derived from the Roman Imperial Baths, contained apses screened by columns and often bookshelves which formed

NEO-CLASSICAL

important architectural elements in themselves. Such was Adam's inventiveness and skill that much intricate interweaving of motifs and ornament on walls and ceilings never became tedious even though a great series of rooms was clearly designed by one creative artist. As his talent matured his plasterwork decorations became shallower and more linear and towards the end of his career his designs could be said to be less serious, more facile. This was not, however, until he had produced many interiors for country houses of the highest merit, Kedleston (from 1759), Syon (1760–9), Osterley (1761–80), Newby (1767–85) and Kenwood (1767–9) being amongst the most prominent. Here he had the opportunity to 'spread' himself and even though he was sometimes confined within an existing shell of earlier date this offered a challenge which he enjoyed, just as at a later date he was able to manipulate magnificent schemes of interior decoration within the confines of narrow London house sites providing the illusion of spatial infinity even rivalling Kent's triumph in Berkeley Square of some thirty years before.

Adam fits into the Neo-classical picture with deliberate and calculating perfection; he could purvey dazzling decoration schemes with his own individual translations of antique ornament; at Culzean Castle (1777–90) he flirted with and ante-dated the growing interest in neo-Gothic Picturesque (but retained a regular façade with a Classical interior) and could provide Edinburgh with a university building of great distinction. He never attempted to upset the traditional demands of civilised patrons but offered a refinement of earlier styles and a Classicism without the Romantic irregularities that his successors were to provide to satisfy the ideals of the Picturesque. And yet, in achieving supreme elegance, Adam failed to produce strength or nobility – two of the most important elements in Greek and Imperial Roman architecture. As Dr Pevsner has asked: 'Where in Adam's work is the severe nobility of Athens or the sturdy virility of Rome?' His leadership of the English Neo-classical movement is based on other, less fundamental things, less true to Greece and Rome than his predecessors but more suited to the sophisticated demands of his clients. His brilliant use of ornament was his answer to Burlington's intellectual dogma.

This therefore left the Greek field wide open to James 'Athenian' Stuart (1713–88) who by the mid-1750s had fully assimilated Winckelmann's doctrine when, with his friend Nicholas Revett, he visited Greece and later published the *Antiquities of Athens*. Had Stuart been endowed with Adam's drive and ambition he might have led a strong anti-Roman movement in England, dear to the hearts of the 'Greek' Neo-classicists; but he was weak and unreliable, a poor disciple for Winckelmann (who, in fact, had no great regard for the *Antiquities*), and apart from influencing interior decoration to a certain degree, his fame must rest on his historic design for the Greek temple at Hagley Hall, Worcestershire (1758), which is considered to be the earliest Doric Revival building in Europe. So the picture was stolen by Adam who had many more attractive things to sell and an eager market awaiting them.

Although Adam produced schemes of overall decoration, he was far from the French Neo-classical ideal on many occasions; wall treatments did not correspond with that of ceilings, pilasters did not support entablatures; often a ceiling would be the sole elaboration in a room, or a fireplace or a chimney-piece; each would be an admirable piece of

opposite. *The Pavillon de Musique de Madame, Versailles, France. Completed in 1781, this little building in the park of Versailles has scenic paintings of charming fantasy in the rotunda*

design in itself but little to do with Clérisseau or Soufflot. These isolated decorations were, however, to have enormous influence in the civilised world and would last appear in America as handsome embellishments to otherwise severely Classical houses. Adam's unifying element was often colour as opposed to design, almost always of soft pastel shades of greens, fawns, pinks and mauves with enrichments in white or gold. This slender medium might have been dismissed as too feminine and weak were it not for the brilliance of its use; in rooms where less overall decoration was employed, walls were sometimes left plain, painted in the predominant colour of the scheme or hung with tapestry or damask, allowing the ceiling and carpet to echo each other's design and to supply decorative interest. But it is in the great rooms where walls, ceilings, carpets, curtains, furniture are designed as a whole that we marvel at Adam's ability to devise displays of amazing originality. Wyatt could do the same when he wanted to (though he professed to dislike Adam's work) but he had not the same powers of concentration or sufficient single-mindedness to rival Adam's output.

Nevertheless Wyatt's output was also enormous and he produced some of the loveliest rooms we know, notably at Heveningham and possibly the dining-room at Crichel; he made another whole career of neo-Gothic houses, the most celebrated being Beckford's ill-fated Fonthill. The distinguished classicist Henry Holland (1745–1806) also played an important rôle and produced interiors which, although much influenced by Adam, adhered to the French Neo-classic principle of ordered sumptuousness inspired by his studies in Paris.

To anyone unfamiliar with the traditions of eighteenth-century domestic architecture Adam's great interiors would come as a surprise when considering the façades behind which they are hidden; few give any idea of the sumptuous scenes within and the rather drab garden front of Kenwood gives no hint of its library, perhaps the finest room of its date in Europe. Nor would the exterior of old Derby House in Grosvenor Square have suggested the miracles of planning and design that Adam devised there. The exteriors of his buildings owed little to the Neo-classical doctrine; sometimes he pasted thin decorated pilasters (similar to those used in the library at Osterley) on his brick façades as at the Adelphi and elsewhere, bringing a little of the interior out-of-doors, but on the whole they are pale reflections of the Palladian tradition and ostentatious exteriors had been left far behind at Sans Souci and Queluz.

Paradoxes of English Neo-classcism were its *Chinoiserie* and neo-Gothic manifestations, *Chinoiserie* was a sporadic expression of English Rococo, used mostly by Chippendale for furniture, but seen at its most fantastic at Claydon where, in the late 1760s, rooms decorated in the most elaborate manner are found side by side with rooms of Palladian gravity.

Neo-Gothic was a small part of Adam's repertoire, but pursued tenaciously by others. In France Soufflot aimed at Roman symmetry and grandeur combined with the *structural lightness* found in Gothic buildings but that is as far as the style was taken in serious French Neo-classicism. In England, however, the Gothic idiom for building and decoration took firm hold on the imagination of those who wanted an alternative to Classicism and sometimes expressed itself in a spirit of Rococo fantasy. Occasionally the interiors would owe a

opposite. The royal visitors' suite, Stockholm Royal Palace. This suite of little rooms with low ceilings contrasts with the sombre grandeur of the state apartments

NEO-CLASSICAL

little of their decorations to structural matters, as in the hall at Fonthill, but in the main Gothic ornament was encrusted over the ceilings and walls of rooms of Classical shape to be enjoyed entirely for its own lively sake – in direct opposition to Neo-classical rules. Such a case is Arbury, where the astounding plaster fan-vaulted decorations have, of course, little or nothing to do with the structure of the rooms and where only the hall possesses an architectural quality. The salon (from 1776) contains plaster vaulting and pendants of incredible intricacy and the library (resembling the one at Strawberry Hill, the ancestor of neo-Gothic invention) has Gothic plasterwork on the walls surrounding the bookshelves; but the painted barrel ceiling takes us back to Etruscan Rome. James Wyatt's Lee Priory (now vanished) less decorated and more architectural, reminds us that neo-Gothic was a serious force by the 1770s and was to be adopted and purveyed in different forms by Nash and others who led the Picturesque movement.

But even with Wyatt as a rival and younger architects rising around him, it is Adam who takes charge of the English Neo-classical scene and not only influences his countrymen but buildings and the use of ornament far beyond the seas, in Italy, France and Russia.

The Adam style in Russia was established in St Petersburg by another Scot, Charles Cameron (c. 1740–1812) who had studied in Rome in the late 1760s. His great interiors for Catherine the Great's Tsarskoe Selo Palace of the early 1780s show Cameron influenced by the earlier, less facile Adam with decorations of a restrained but robust Classicism and his 'Grecian' Hall at the Pavlovsk Palace of the same date takes us back nearly twenty years to the alabaster columns in the hall at Kedleston.

America In America, yet another form of Neo-classicism was emerging late in the day. Until the 1770s American interiors were very much the product of a cultural life dependent on England and most of the decorations and embellishments of rooms were inspired by or copied from the standard design books of Gibbs, Langley and Morris. A time-lag was inevitable and Langley's *City and Country Builders' Treasury* (1756) was being used at Mount Vernon as late as 1780. The distance from England and, at first, the limited amount of money available tended to result in houses where comfort and dignity prevailed. They were attractive Queen Anne or 'Georgian' buildings, out of fashion by English standards, but eminently pleasing and civilised.

Wood panelling, abandoned in England at the beginning of the eighteenth century in favour of plastered walls, was universal in America until the mid-1770s except in certain cases in New York and Pennsylvania where plastered walls arrived earlier. Wood was, in any case, the most plentiful and the cheapest building material to hand and with it grew up an excellent tradition in joinery. These early panelled rooms were quite simple affairs with little ornament other than perhaps a dentilled cornice and Roman Doric pilasters framing a chimney breast. Certain salient parts of a room such as door and window frames were considered legitimate subjects for elaboration but even at a much later date American rooms never adopted the complex, grotesque and arabesque-laden decorations of France and England; many important rooms had absolutely bare walls with elaborate plaster ceil-

The third drawing room at Derby House, Grosvenor Square, London, designed by Robert Adam in 1773–4. The beautiful and detailed engraving gives a rare view of the gorgeous interior of this vanished house. Nevertheless a slightly creepy atmosphere pervades this cool essay in geometric form, devoid of furniture and people, and bathed in what might be moonlight

ings and richly designed fireplaces, often gaining immensely in effect by this selectiveness.

One suspects that this attention to certain decorative elements was partly due to the fact that references for such designs were illustrated separately in the pattern books, designed by different people, often at different times. Besides, a rich man might import a chimney-piece from England at some expense and wish to give it place of honour in a room, uncluttered by other detail. Chimney-pieces were almost always in wood or plaster unless imported and often very elaborate, sometimes containing looking-glasses or paintings and topped by a triangular or broken pediment. The common placing of chimneys between rooms or on exterior walls gave opportunity for the deep recesses on either side to be filled with arches and doors or windows. Ceilings were at first Rococo in feeling, derived from Gibbs and Langley; it is not until after 1775 that we see the influence of Adam, and the Frenchmen who supplied the ceilings at Kenmore were itinerant, providing an exceptional glimpse of sumptuousness. But until the last ten years of the century architecture and decoration in America never loses a Palladian tenor except for an occasional excursion into Chippendale-inspired *Chinoiserie*.

But all this was before anything approaching Neo-classicism, as understood by continental designers, reached America towards the end of the century and Peter Harrison (1716–75), an English amateur, was the leading light in these early days, basing all his knowledge on English Palladian and earlier principles with scholarship and understanding. There were several others, too, who followed him and produced buildings of much distinction.

In the 1790s, Charles Bulfinch (1763–1844) had returned to America from studies in England, France and Italy and soon established himself as an expert and prolific Neo-classicist and slavish follower of Adam. His contemporary Samuel McIntire carried the

NEO-CLASSICAL

development of American architectural style still further and produced a series of magnificent mansions in New England – with decorations directly inspired by Adam but so disposed as to create a refreshingly original concept of the Classical theme.

But it was the War of American Independence that marked the point at which American architecture begins to assert itself in its own right, and towering above mere architects, was the austere figure of architect, lawyer, politician and future President of the United States, Thomas Jefferson (1743–1826). He, too, had studied in England, France and Italy and had returned full of enthusiasm for the Roman ruins at Nîmes and the English-inspired Palladian buildings of Paris. His influence, however, mainly affected official buildings where he established a personal form of Classicism which, as Sir John Summerson has made clear, was based on Palladianism; but not on the Palladianism of Burlington but that of the buildings he so much admired in France. He professed extreme distaste for everything he saw in England even though Clérisseau was his mentor in Paris – the very man who had inspired and encouraged so much of what he found distasteful!

It was, therefore, the followers of the English school who set the pattern of American domestic design which culminated in the Greek Revival and is represented, for many years after the turn of the century, by the articulate buildings and elegant rooms we connect with plantation houses – long after the dates covering the mainstream of European Neo-classicism.

Engraving of a fête at the Pavillon Du Barry given in honour of the King in 1771. This very strictly architectural little house was built by C. N. Ledoux for Madame Du Barry at Louveciennes

Section showing the back wall of the Porters' Hall, Shelburne (later Lansdowne) House, Berkeley Square, London. This lovely engraving shows the masters in their more severe manner. Nevertheless their skill is immediately evident, cool, strict, erudite and imaginative. From 'The Works in Architecture of Robert and James Adam Esquires', London 1779

Grand Salon in the Hôtel de Monaco, rue St Dominique, Paris: a design by A. T. Brongniard in 1776

Château du Champs de Bataille, near Le Neubourg, France

above and opposite. The grand vestibule on the first floor: a strict and architectural scheme of decoration, formal and rather cold, but very impressive. The castle was built in 1606–1701, but this room was redecorated towards the end of the eighteenth century

Haga Slot, near Stockholm

opposite. *Bedroom in the little castle built for King Gustavus III in 1786–8. The interior has charming rooms in the contemporary French manner*

Hammond–Harwood House, Annapolis, Maryland, USA

The dining room, built in about 1775 by the architect William Buckland, is very representative of the prosperous American interior of this period

The ballroom at Lazienki, Poland. This delightful palace, built on an artificial island in the middle of a river, was constructed to the designs of Domenico Merlini for Stanislas, the last King of Poland. This room, in the international style of the time, was finished in about 1790

Opposite. Reception room at Haga Slot, near Stockholm, 1788

Library at Drottningholm, Sweden. Originally built at the end of the seventeenth century by Nicodemus Tessin, large parts of the interior were decorated in the second half of the eighteenth century and this room dates from about 1760

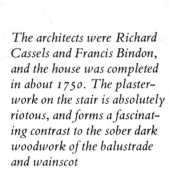

The architects were Richard Cassels and Francis Bindon, and the house was completed in about 1750. The plasterwork on the stair is absolutely riotous, and forms a fascinating contrast to the sober dark woodwork of the balustrade and wainscot

Detail of one of the carved fireplace panels

opposite. The Salon at Russborough. Elaborate plasterwork, mahogany woodwork, dark red cut velvet wall hangings make up an interior of great richness

Russborough, County Wicklow, Ireland

Palais Abbatial de Royaumont, Ile-de-France

above. *The first floor hall*

left. *The lower hall. The architect was Louis Le Masson, a follower of Ledoux, and the interior was completed in 1789*

Schloss Benrath, near Düsseldorf, Germany

above right. *The Kuppelsaal. Begun in 1756 for the Elector Palatine Charles Theodore, the interior of the castle was complete by 1771. Domed interiors were very popular in eighteenth-century Germany*

right. *Detail of the eye of the cupola at Benrath, with a fanciful painting of putti folding up a net*

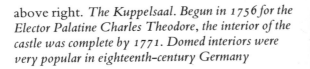

Château de Versailles, France

The octagonal salon, Pavillon de Musique de Madame. This room lies behind the circular room with the painted walls, and forms a brilliant contrast. The richness and refinement of the carving may be compared with that of the Salon de M. le Prince at Chantilly.

Royal Palace, Caserta, Italy

above. *The first landing*

left. *The Palace was begun in 1760 to the designs of Luigi Vanvitelli and the most remarkable feature of the interior is the grand staircase, which affords a constantly changing series of complex vistas*

opposite. *One of the stone lions guarding the first flight of steps*

The entrance hall, Heveningham Hall, Norfolk, England. James Wyatt designed this beautiful bland composition, and it was completed about 1781. This room is undoubtedly one of the most important Classic Revival interiors in England

opposite. The Salon, Castle Coole, Co. Fermanagh, Ireland. Designed for Lord Belmore by James Wyatt, and built between 1788 and 1798, this house is perhaps the most perfect example of the English Neo-classical style of the late eighteenth century. The state rooms are laid out with perfect symmetry along the north front, but the most attractive of them is the central circular salon linking the dining room and the drawing room

Kenwood, London

Opposite. The library designed by Robert Adam for Lord Mansfield and completed in 1768. This is a particularly characteristic Adam interior and is one of his great triumphs. Plaster arabesques by Joseph Rose, ceiling paintings by Zucchi, screens of columns, a barrel ceiling, semi-domes – all the details, tricks and elements that are associated with his designs are here combined in a composition of true genius

right. Detail of the white marble fireplace and gilt framed over-mantel glass at Kenwood

ROMANTIC REVIVAL 1790-1840

Peter Fleetwood-Hesketh

The fifty years that followed the fall of the Bastille probably witnessed more fundamental changes in the western world than may be found in any similar span of its known history. In a sense, the years 1790–1840, an era that embraced the death of Catherine the Great and the earliest writings of Karl Marx, form a bridge between an old world with which we now have relatively little in common and the modern one in which we live.

The liberal thoughts and ideals that had been forming through the eighteenth century, the desire for emancipation from the established order, had already found significant expression in the American colonies' unilateral declaration of independence in 1776. In France, accumulating discontent finally erupted in a violent and tragic revolution which began in 1789 and reached its terrible end in 1793. The aftermath was the rise to power of a military dictator who for twenty-two years ravaged Europe with war, from Cadiz to Moscow, from the Netherlands to the Nile.

Meanwhile, symptoms of change, superficial perhaps, are discernible in minor ways, even, for example, in the dress of the period, in which many of the trappings and symbols of an old régime seem suddenly to have vanished. Men's dress has become more subdued in colour. Simply cut clothes of plain material have replaced the richly brocaded garments of earlier days and gone are their frills and lace. Wigs, which had been diminishing in size for a hundred years, are now cast aside by all except the legal profession.

Contemporary thought and philosophy were reflected in the arts, especially in architecture. On the one hand there were serious attempts to interpret and express revolutionary ideas, 'rationalism' and a break with tradition; on the other, a romantic and sometimes frivolous mood of make-believe, which looked back into a remote and largely imaginary past, or out towards distant and little-known lands – first China, then Egypt and India.

To account for all that happened in the sphere of design and decoration in this period, we have to look back a little way into the ideas that had been formulating during the previous half-century, for it was then that the architectural revolution began.

The emancipation of architectural thought in Europe from the Roman Classic tradition, Palladian as well as Baroque, becomes perceptible in the middle of the eighteenth century

opposite. *The Goya Salon at the Palacio Liria, Madrid, Spain. This interior is notable for its collection of Goya paintings, all dating from the late eighteenth or early nineteenth centuries. Also noteworthy is the enormous Empire desk encrusted with ormolu mounts in the strictest 'Romantic Classical' taste*

and was complete before its end. It is seen in an increasing desire to exploit the possibilities of other historic but hitherto forgotten or neglected styles – not only Greek and Gothic, but also those of the east – as well as such variations of Classic as may be seen in the art of ancient Pompeii and Etruria and in its early Italian renaissance. In the process, architecture lost some of the spontaneity inherent in a strong tradition and became more self-conscious.

But in spite of this great diversity of thoughts and trends, European architecture remained generally Classic, with Gothic, its only serious rival, still confined mainly to England and, in a lesser degree, to northern Germany.

Styles and Trends

ROMANTIC CLASSIC

The growing interest in archaeological research was no doubt at first inspired by the paintings of Classical ruins by seventeenth-century French artists such as Nicolas Poussin, Claude Lorrain and Pierre Patel the elder.

The excavation of Roman antiquities began at Herculaneum in 1709 and at Pompeii in 1748. In 1753 Robert Wood (1717–71) published his *Ruins of Palmyra*; J.D.Leroy (1724–1803) his studies of Grecian ruins in 1758 which were followed by those of James Stuart (1713–88) and Nicholas Revett (1720–1804) in 1762.

In 1764 Robert Adam, whose works had a notable influence upon the course of European architecture, brought out his book on the ruins of Diocletian's palace at Spalato, and fourteen years later Charles-Louis Clérisseau, who had worked with Adam, produced his *Antiquities of Nîmes*, which was republished in 1804.

From these antiquarian studies sprang the Romantic Classicism which dominated the latter part of the eighteenth century and continued well into the nineteenth. It finds expression in the paintings of Hubert Robert and the etchings of G. B. Piranesi.

ORIGINS OF MODERN DESIGN

Simultaneously we find a new abstract, geometrical approach to architecture, notably in the designs of two Frenchmen, E.L.Boullée (1728–99) and Claude-Nicolas Ledoux (1736–1806); in the works of David Gilly (1748–1808) in Berlin and of his son Friedrich (1772–1800) and of Sir John Soane (1753–1837) in England.

They aimed at simplicity and clarity, relying for their effects upon the juxtaposition of elementary geometric forms and the play of light upon their surfaces. They sought greater variety in the use of shapes and spaces, both externally and internally, so that by means of vaults and apses, screens and sometimes partly hidden recesses, rooms became very much more interesting. Moreover, the sequences in which they were arranged were designed to provide contrast and variety in passing from one to another, while the best advantage was taken of every opportunity to create vistas and perspectives.

NATIONAL AND INTERNATIONAL

Although during the period with which we are now concerned, the domestic interiors of different European countries are in some cases distinguished by certain national qualities – the crystalline hardness found in France, the fine attenuated linear character in northern

Germany or that of solid comfort in England – many more reveal little or nothing which indicates at a glance their country of origin. And there are many features that are common to all and that seem to belong especially to this period.

The most universal idiom was basically Greco-Roman, most typically seen, for example, in many of the works of Charles Percier (1764–1838) and his partner Pierre Léonard Fontaine (1762–1853) in France, of Leo von Klenze (1784–1864) in Bavaria and of their equivalents in other countries.

Its elements are based upon antique forms, handled with great assurance and dexterity – columns, pilasters and entablatures; medallions, arabesques, wreaths and caryatid figures. To these in due course were added Egyptian sphinxes, Napoleonic eagles and the swan motif in furniture. Meanwhile, entirely new proportions were introduced when Pompeiian wall decoration was translated into three-dimensional form, with its slender rod-like columns, suggestive of metal or wood, and other attenuated features.

DÉCOR

These decorations were frequently gilt upon a white or tinted ground; sometimes, alternatively, bronze green. The ornamental detail, usually in low relief, is so fine and sharp that it becomes difficult to distinguish between what is in reality gilded or bronzed plaster or wood and that which is of the metal itself.

Great use was made of marble, scagliola, graining and marbling. Large mirrors were introduced, and placed where they would be architecturally most effective. Illumination was by means of candelabra, torchères and large circular chandeliers, hung from shallow-coffered ceilings. Communicating doors became higher and wider, and folding double doors became usual even between small rooms.

At first there was a tendency towards a frigid formality; a certain stiffness and austerity of line, in contrast to the easy grace of former years. But this was gradually relaxed, as will be seen.

This was the great age of the collector of classical antiquities, like Charles Towneley and Henry Blundell. Greek and Roman statues, busts and medallions were freely used for their decorative value, both the ancient originals and modern imitations. The principal variants of Classical decoration are to be seen in the Greek and Egyptian furnishings designed by Thomas Hope of Deepdene (1769–1831), in the Pompeiian decoration of Percier and Fontaine in France and of their contemporaries throughout Europe.

FURNITURE AND FURNISHINGS

In the 1790s furniture had reached the height of sophisticated simplicity. Many pieces of this period have the fine workmanship and subtle curvature of contemporary coachbuilding, often possessing far greater strength than their slenderness might suggest. At the same time an increasing degree of ingenuity was exercised in combining elegance with utility.

About 1800 the furnishing of rooms began gradually to become more luxurious, more massive and more upholstered. Sofas, built against the wall or in corners, and sometimes solid down to the floor, were provided with fitted bolsters and cushions, often of very

ROMANTIC REVIVAL

rich materials, tasselled and fringed, and with tables specially designed in conjunction with them, often supported by one large central leg instead of smaller ones at the corners.

Walls were lined with silk, and interiors came to depend more upon the richness of their furnishings than on decoration applied to their walls. Draperies became more profuse, a draped pole often extending over several windows, and hangings were sometimes continued round the walls, an idea no doubt originally derived from Pompeiian decoration. Deep fringes, were made of elaborately turned, silk-covered wooden bobbins (craftsmanship was already becoming mechanised). Silken ropes were used for bell-pulls and to hang pictures; chandelier-chains were draped in silk. Rooms were more sumptuously carpeted and there was more glitter and more gilding, much of it highly burnished.

These tendencies are nowhere better illustrated than in the long-vanished interiors of Carlton House in London. The restoration of this Palladian house was begun for the Prince Regent by Henry Holland in 1783, and by 1790 was sufficiently advanced to enable the Regent to hold a levée there on 8 February that year. The work was later continued by James Wyatt and John Nash, and furnished in the style made popular by George Smith, who, as 'Upholder to His Royal Highness the Prince of Wales', published his *Collection of Designs for Household Furniture and Interior Decoration* in 1805. The interiors of Carlton House, beautifully illustrated in W. H. Pyne's *Royal Residences* (1819) undoubtedly had a great influence on contemporary taste.

In the ensuing years, rooms that had before been relatively sparsely furnished became filled with an increasingly varied assortment of objects; commodes and vitrines, ottomans, stools and chaises-longues, *jardinières* and *chiffoniers*; clocks under glass domes, flanked by vases, torchères or statuettes. Mantelpieces were made deeper to allow room for these *garnitures de cheminées*. People formed collections of coins, minerals, birds, butterflies, shells or eggs. The tops of small tables were sometimes inlaid with samples of different kinds of marble, and provided with a diagram giving the name of each.

There was greater variety in the use of woods and veneers in the manufacture of furniture – maple and satinwood, often inlaid, painted or gilt; and light oak or bamboo, both real and imitation. More rosewood, frequently inlaid with brass, was used for furniture in place of mahogany, but white and gold or solidly gilt furniture remained fashionable; while in 'Biedermeier' we find a reaction towards greater simplicity.

The early years of the nineteenth century brought an increasing desire to unite 'out-of-doors' with 'indoors'. Windows were made larger, their sills cut lower, or made as 'French' windows giving direct access to the garden or terrace, and the view through them became more consciously part of the design. Rooms opened into winter-gardens and conservatories, such as that built for George IV in cast iron Gothic by Thomas Hopper (1776–1856) at Carlton House.

In some cases, for example at the Ajuda Palace in Lisbon, rooms within the main structure were filled with ornamental vegetation of various sorts. An outdoor effect was sometimes achieved by using trellis, and aviaries were much in vogue. There was also a fashion, especially popular in France, for scenic wallpaper, representing a continuous landscape round the entire walls of a room.

While marble and scagliola were extensively used, silk or paper continued as the normal covering for walls, the former usually surrounded by a gilt moulding covering the nails with which it was fixed, the latter sometimes provided with a printed border.

In addition to the larger paintings placed for their architectural effect, smaller ones were often arranged in closely spaced groups or horizontal rows. A fashion sometimes observed in rooms of the early nineteenth century, possibly to create an illusion of extra height, was to omit the dado or chair rail that had been *de rigueur* throughout the eighteenth.

By the 1830s, industrial methods were already affecting design. As candles were superseded by oil and gas, fittings were designed to suit these lighting methods, with opaque glass shades and round or tulip-shaped globes.

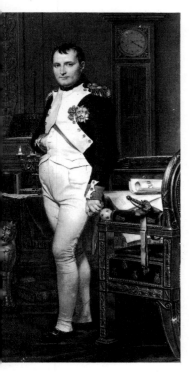

Napoleon in his Study, by Jacques-Louis David, 1812. Given in a picture showing so little of the room, the architectural qualities of the Empire style are very apparent: the rigid form of the clock-case, the leopard-legged desk and the chair like a Roman throne

France

In the architecture of post-revolutionary France, no two names are more famous than those of the partnership of Charles Percier and Pierre Léonard Fontaine, perhaps France's greatest exponents of the current idiom. Their work is to be seen at Malmaison, where the Empress Josephine's round bedroom is hung with crimson drapery between slender gilded columns, and Napoleon's library, whose segmental vaulting is supported on columns that rest on plinths of dado height. For Fontainebleau Percier designed and Georges Jacob (1739–1814) made the Emperor's throne, beneath a draped canopy, flanked by eagles.

The larger scale interiors of Percier and Fontaine, such as we find in the Louvre or in the Palace of Versailles, have nothing like the charm and variety of their smaller, more intimate rooms like those at Malmaison and elsewhere.

Among the innumerable other architects working in France at this time may be mentioned Boullée's pupil Marie-Joseph Peyre (1770–1843), who was also both Percier and Fontaine's master, and L. M. Berthault (*c.* 1771–1823) who worked for Madame Récamier. Others included Brongniard (1739–1813), M. Crucy (1749–1826) and A. Vaudoyer (1756–1846), to be followed by J. I. Hittorff (1793–1867) and Percier's brilliant pupil L. J. Duc (1802–79), a French equivalent of England's C. R. Cockerell.

Among the better known cabinet makers were Georges Jacob, Arnoult, Bellangé, Mauter, Lemarchand, Lesage, Biennais and Alphonse Jacob-Desmalter. These *ébénistes* worked in the tradition of Riesener but introduced many inventions of their own. Much of their furniture is of rosewood, or ebonised, and decorated with brass inlays and mounts, and was generally designed to be complementary to its architectural setting.

In general, the characteristic style of the Directoire and Empire shows a distinct and probably deliberate change from the more conservative and traditional idiom of pre-Revolutionary days. A new, bourgeois patronage demanded greater comfort; less tradition and formality. It is much more Pompeiian in feeling, and introduces new, sometimes topical features such as sphinxes and other Egyptian motifs. Stars, eagles, fasces and palms were much used, as well as Pompeiian tent-like draperies and garlands.

Henceforward, taste in France changed little, developing on lines parallel with those followed in other European countries. Under the restored monarchy, there was a partial

ROMANTIC REVIVAL

reversion to the fashions prevalent in the reign of Louis XVI, but lacking some of their refinement. Gothic became fashionable with Hittorff's decorations designed for the coronation of Charles X in 1824, but the Greco-Roman that had become traditional remained the dominant style, though a little heavier in treatment.

Great Britain Robert Adam died in 1792; his brothers James and William, respectively, in 1794 and 1815. They had in the 1760s introduced a style of Classic interior whose influence swept over Europe and which remained, in its different variations, the absolute convention until the end of the century. Sir William Chambers (1723–96) was almost the only one of their older contemporaries to resist the fashion set by them. Among the younger, Samuel Wyatt (1737–1807) and his brother James (1746–1813), accepted it with enthusiasm and developed it in a distinctive manner of their own, as may be seen at Heveningham Hall in Suffolk (1788–9), Dodington Park, Gloucestershire (1798–1808), these by James; Tatton Park in Cheshire (c. 1805) by Samuel, and in the fine interiors of Liverpool Town Hall (1795–7) by James in conjunction with John Foster.

Samuel and James Wyatt belonged to a very large family which in four generations produced no fewer than nineteen architects. Almost contemporary with Samuel and James, two men stand out as somewhat divergent from the prevailing Adam convention.

The first of these was Henry Holland (1745–1806) who developed a rather subtle Greco-Roman manner of his own, based upon a close study of contemporary French interiors. There is a peaceful simplicity about his rooms which sometimes have gently rounded corners and invariably exquisite details. He had undertaken many important commissions before 1790, including interiors at Carlton House and Althorp, and in 1795 rebuilt Southill House in Bedfordshire for Samuel Whitbread.

Further away from accepted fashion was Sir John Soane (1753–1837), who for six years had worked as Holland's assistant. Soane was clearly much influenced by the work of the younger George Dance (1741–1825) to whom he was apprenticed from the age of fifteen. He developed the somewhat ascetic style, originated by Dance, in which many of the conventional elements of Greco-Roman architecture were eliminated and replaced by frets and grooves, while those retained were of unorthodox design. He made great use of shallow saucer domes, clerestory lighting, and segmental arches, sometimes in the form of pendants. For ornament he had a fondness for sepulchral emblems – wreaths, sarcophagi and cinerary urns.

Soane's most important interiors were those executed for the Bank of England between 1788 and 1833; his most charming, perhaps, those at Wimpole in Cambridgeshire, 1791–93; his most original – almost sinister – those in his own house at 13 Lincoln's Inn Fields, London, now the Sir John Soane Museum.

The vogue for non-European styles found flamboyant expression at Sezincote (Gloucestershire), designed in an Indian style about 1805 by Samuel Pepys Cockerell (c. 1754–1827) who took his details from the aquatints of Thomas Daniell (1749–1840) and his brothers; and at the Pavilion at Brighton (1815–21), that Indo-Chinese-Gothic cocktail,

left. The 'Platinum room' in the Casita del Labrador at Aranjuez, Spain, c. 1810. This incredibly rich interior was designed by Percier and Fontaine for Joseph Bonaparte, King of Spain. The walls were mahogany with platinum ornaments, inset panels painted by Girodet, and looking-glasses set into the compartments of the arch tympanum and beside the door. This kind of inventiveness easily disposes of these architects' reputation for coldness and academicism

below. The picture gallery, in the house of Thomas Hope in Duchess St, London, built to his own design in 1820. The house, originally built by Adam, was completely altered internally by Hope, and the gallery, grand, strict and very impressive, is a typical example of the designing skill of this gifted and influential amateur

Gallery at No. 14 Regent Street, London, built for himself by the architect John Nash and completed in 1824. This magnificent apartment was one of the reception rooms on the first floor of the house, and served as a processional way between the drawing room and the dining room; it was some seventy feet long

mixed for the Prince Regent by his architect John Nash (1752–1835). No architect of the Georgian era left a more conspicuous mark upon its closing decades.

Although already in practice in London and in Wales by 1777, it was not until the turn of the century that the patronage of the Prince of Wales (later King George IV) gave to Nash the great opportunities he was able so triumphantly to exploit. He was a master planner, both of houses and of streets, and in the latter sphere his major work was the formation of Regent Street and Regent's Park in London, between the years 1812 and 1830.

For his royal patron in 1813 he remodelled the ground storey of Carlton House; and between 1815 and 1821 the Pavilion at Brighton in fantastic oriental style. From 1825 to 1830 Buckingham House was rebuilt as Buckingham Palace from Nash's designs and its rich Classic interiors are among the most beautiful in the kingdom.

Sir Jeffry Wyatville (1766–1840) was a nephew of Samuel and James Wyatt. Between 1820 and 1840 he made extensive alterations and additions at Chatsworth and from 1824 until 1836 was engaged at Windsor Castle, where his interiors sounded the keynote for all that was most sumptuous in early Victorian England. No less magnificent, however, were those designed by his cousin Benjamin Dean Wyatt (1775–1850) who, with his brother Philip, completed York (now Lancaster) House in 1825–6 and added the Waterloo Gallery to Apsley House. The style is an adaptation of French *Régence*.

Among the finest of the later English Classic rooms must be included Sir Robert Smirke's 'King's Library' in the British Museum, c. 1830; Philip Hardwick's Goldsmiths' Hall, 1829–35, and the interiors of the Travellers' and Reform Clubs, c. 1830 and 1837 respectively, by Sir Charles Barry (1795–1860). The great galleried central hall of the latter – a roofed and top lit *cortile*, the first of its kind – is one of the grandest rooms in London, and both clubs have long libraries sub-divided by small columns upon plinths.

Barry is, however, best known as the architect of the Palace of Westminster, begun in 1836 and by far the largest building yet produced in the Gothic Revival, in which he entrusted all the decoration to the dexterous hands and almost fanatical mind of Augustus Welby Northmore Pugin (1812–52).

The Romantic Revival of Gothic architecture probably emanated from meditations upon a legendary past, similar to those that inspired the novels of Sir Walter Scott and were satirized in those of Thomas Love Peacock. This could account for the ancient (and modern) arms and armour that came to clutter the halls of many a stately home, and for the growing interest in heraldry, that duly found its way into the stained glass of their lofty traceried windows. No doubt it was upon ideas such as these, coupled with a painter's eye for the picturesque, that castles like Gwrych (1814), Belvoir (1801–16) and Margam (1830–5) arose, all of them places as highly Romantic as one could wish for.

Gothic had been practised by James Wyatt, John Nash, Barry and many others. To them it was merely part of their repertoire of various styles, in each of which they could work with equanimity. In Augustus Welby Pugin, however, we find a much more earnest disciple, for to him Gothic was the only acceptable style and he was, indeed, its greatest exponent at that time.

He is best known for the fabulous Gothic dress in which he clothed Barry's Houses of

The breakfast room in the
house of Sir John Soane, at 13
Lincoln's Inn Fields, London,
1812. This curious little
room, in the fascinating house
built for himself by one of
England's greatest architects,
is one of the most remarkable
domestic interiors in the
world. The spatial relationships of the hanging dome and
the barrel-vault toplights, the
unexpected views across the
courtyard and into other
rooms, the use of mirrors to
break down the apparent
solidity of walls – these and
many other devices produce
an effect of complete fantasy

Parliament. Of his domestic interiors, the best that survive, though no longer complete in every detail, are those at Scarisbrick Hall in Lancashire, 1836–45. Under Pugin's influence the 'Gothick' of the eighteenth century, such as we see at Laycock, Arbury or Birr Castle, moved steadily on towards the neo-Gothic of the nineteenth.

Meanwhile, Charles Robert Cockerell (1788–1863) was developing a highly individual Classic Neo-Grec of his own; William Burn (1789–1870), in the late 1830s, co-operated in the Elizabethan fantasy of Harlaxton Manor in Lincolnshire with Antony Salvin (1799–1881), an expert on fortresses who also designed Peckforton Castle in Cheshire, the walls of whose principal rooms are of dressed sandstone. While the firm of Frederick Crace (1779–1857) was much employed for arabesque decoration.

An impression of current English taste and fashions for furniture and interior decoration can be obtained from the volumes of Ackermann's *Repository of Arts*, or designs published by George Smith, while the grandest interiors are illustrated in such works as W. H. Pyne's *Royal Residences* or Joseph Nash's magnificent interior views of Windsor Castle.

Italy Some of Italy's most impressive interiors are to be found in the royal palaces of Caserta and Naples, created for the Bourbon King Ferdinand II. The severely architectural 'Hall of Mars' at Caserta was formed in 1807 by Antonio de Simone. Vast sculptured panels by Valerio Monreale fill the spaces between Ionic pilasters and the same kind of decoration continues over the coved ceiling.

One of the last great rooms to be decorated in the international Empire tradition is the

ROMANTIC REVIVAL

Throne Room at Caserta, decorated in 1839–45 by Gaetano Genovesi (1795–1860) with Angelini and Tommaso Arnaud; a huge room with coupled Corinthian pilasters and an enriched vaulted ceiling pierced by *lunette* windows. Genovesi also redecorated the Throne Room in the Royal Palace at Naples in 1837–42. It has a great coved ceiling with large gilt stucco figures symbolising the provinces of the Kingdom of Naples. Much of the stucco decoration and some of the furniture is the work of Pelagio Palagi, who also decorated many of the rooms in the Royal Palace at Turin.

Though Italy remained a source of inspiration for studying the past, its contemporary architects no longer exercised any international influence, save those who worked abroad, like Quarenghi in Russia. France had for long been the fount of fashion, and French architects and decorators were widely employed all over Europe. For new ideas, however, eyes were now turning more towards England and Germany.

Germany In the central European states the tendency had been to follow the fashion of France. From the *Frühklassicismus* that had been used by Friedrich Wilhelm von Erdmannsdorff at Wörlitz in 1773 and for Frederick the Great's bedroom at Sans Souci in 1786, an adapted version of Empire was evolved. In effecting this evolution the school of Friedrich Weinbrenner of Karlsruhe (1766–1826) had a considerable influence.

The work of Heinrich Gentz (1766–1801) at Weimar and Berlin, of Jussow at Cassel and of Brendel of Potsdam, who in 1794–7 decorated the interior of the little castle on *Pfaueninsel*, belong to this epoch, whose courtly Classicism is epitomised in the *Grosse Saal* of the Palais Prinz Karl in Munich, a charming building of moderate size designed by Karl von Fischer (1782–1820). It has pink scagliola walls, white pilasters and carved gilt doors. The ceiling is painted in flat *grisaille* panels. In the same city Fischer also designed the handsome National Theatre.

The Napoleonic wars had a severely restrictive effect upon building activity which was reduced to a minimum between the battles of Jena in 1806 and Leipzig in 1813.

With the return of peace, one of the most important figures to emerge in early nineteenth-century German architecture was the Hanoverian Leo von Klenze (1784–1864), who became the chief architect of Ludwig I of Bavaria. His buildings have a Roman grandeur to which he applied his own powerful Classic ornament. This has more robustness and clarity than that of Percier and Fontaine.

Some of Klenze's best work was destroyed in the air raids on Munich in 1944, including many of the finest interiors of the Residenz and all those of the Glyptotek. Some of these are being restored. The palace he built for Duke Max of Bavaria in 1822–6 contained interiors of noble and mature quality. It stood in the Ludwigstrasse in Munich but was demolished in 1936.

Klenze was responsible for charming Pompeiian decoration in the castles of Ismaning and Pappenheim, and designed the New Hermitage Museum at St Petersburg.

Turning to Northern Germany, and particularly to Prussia, we find working in Berlin the architects K. G. Langhans (1733–1808) whose Brandenburg Gate (1789–93) is a relatively early essay in Greek Revival; his son K. F. Langhans (1781–1869); David Gilly (1748–1808)

opposite. *The Etruscan room, Castello Reale di Raconigi, near Turin, Italy. The castle was altered and decorated for King Carlo Alberto in 1834 by Pelagio Palagi and Carlo Bellosio, and this little room is one of their happiest inventions*

and his son Friedrich (1772–1800); and Heinrich Gentz (1766–1801).

Destined to achieve greater fame than these was Karl Friedrich Schinkel (1784–1841), a pupil of David Gilly and an associate of his son Friedrich. Schinkel began as a designer of stage sets – his designs for *The Magic Flute* are among the best ever made – and a painter in the German Romantic landscape style of Caspar David Friedrich.

When still quite young, however, he was appointed Chief Court Architect to the King of Prussia, a position he held until his death in 1841. For much of this period he was fortunate in having the best of patrons in the person of the Crown Prince, later King Frederick William IV (1795–1861), himself a talented and imaginative artist and pupil.

Schinkel and the school of architects that he founded gave to the heart of Berlin the architectural character it retained until World War II. Among his many works is the charming little palace of Charlottenhof in the Park of Sans Souci at Potsdam, built in 1826–9 for Prince Frederick William after his marriage to Princess Elisabeth of Bavaria. And for the King he designed the Grecian villa of Orianda on the shores of the Black Sea.

In the Prinz Albrecht Palace in Berlin, Schinkel designed an oval room whose walls were lined with marble and mirrors. Segmental niches were fitted with built-in sofas, while the centre was occupied by a round back-to-back sofa under the central chandelier. In 1825 he designed the round Garten Salon (a small garden temple) in Bellvue Park. Panels of Pompeiian designs painted on paper fill the spaces between Corinthian pilasters that support a dome decorated as a sort of umbrella whose spokes are made of garlands. The arabesque ornament contains medallions and mythical figures.

Schinkel's characteristic decoration has the somewhat tenuous and astringent quality that we find in all his architecture. His ornament is very often painted flat, in colour, on the wall surfaces or mouldings, only the strictly architectural features being three-dimensional. Many of his designs for furniture are extremely delicate, some of it of finely wrought metal. There were also the grander, more formal pieces, incorporating winged sphinxes and other emblems of antiquity.

Although we associate Schinkel with his own and rather special kind of Greco-Roman Classicism, he, like most of his contemporaries, could turn his hand to Gothic when required. Indeed, his taste for Gothic is apparent in the buildings shown in some of his early romantic paintings.

In 1834 he designed the castle of Babelsberg near Potsdam in 'English Tudor' for Prince William of Prussia, afterwards William I (1797–1888). The rib-vaulted ceiling of its octagonal ballroom is supported on clustered columns and painted with arabesques. The *tee-salon* is also octagonal. Its pointed french windows open upon a grassy slope that goes down to the Jungfernsee. Schinkel's other great Gothic castle is Stolzenfels on the Rhine.

Meanwhile his pupil, Ludwig Persius, who designed many charming Italianate buildings at Potsdam for Frederick William IV, was also quite willing to attempt other styles, and designed a suite of rooms in revived Rococo for Sans Souci.

Of the various royal palaces in Berlin, the most distinguished, though by no means the largest, was that built in Unter den Linden for Prince William at the same time as Babelsberg. It was designed in Schinkel's mature neo-Classic manner and executed by

opposite. *Josephine's bedroom, Château de Malmaison, France. This fantastic room was decorated in 1810 by Percier and Fontaine for the Empress Josephine when she took up residence in the house after her divorce. The tent form was a particular favourite of the period*

K. F. Langhans (the younger). It contained a staircase guarded by winged angels which led to a round ballroom whose Corinthian columns supported a gallery with a low dome.

The Prince died as Emperor in 1888 and his widow, the Kaiserin Augusta, lived on in the palace until her own death. A portrait painted in 1890 shows her as an old lady with a charming, pensive expression. Thereafter these grand but comfortable interiors were kept as a museum, in every detail exactly as he and she had lived in and left them, much as Osborne is to this day.

The building was burnt out in World War II, and its rooms can now only be seen in photographs or drawings, or through the aquatints meticulously made when they were lived in and cherished. When we look into them we are looking into a world and a life which in the span of a single generation has utterly vanished. The façade of the palace remains and has been restored, though shorn of the proud eagles that stood at each end. All behind it is new.

Other countries in Western Europe

A general survey of other Western European countries reveals no great differences in the design of interiors during the period under review.

Some examples are certainly worth mentioning, such as those in the Royal Palace of Madrid, the Casita del Principe, Escorial, or the Casita del Labrador at Aranjuez in Spain. This small palace was built in 1792–1803 for Charles IV and Maria Luisa, by Isidro Gonzàles Velàzquez. The highly ornamented walls of the dining room are divided into a rich pattern of small panels of flattened octagonal shape, containing landscape and seascape paintings.

The ballroom is similar in treatment. Under a great painted ceiling the walls are decorated with Pompeiian plaques, round, octagonal and oblong, depicting running and dancing figures and set in a rich mass of arabesque ornament.

Examples in Holland, especially during the reign of Louis Buonaparte who was King of Holland from 1806 till 1810, are similar to those of France: the Royal Palace in the Hague was furnished by Thomire, Cuel and the Dutchman Breytspraak. The same may be said of Belgium and the Scandinavian countries.

America

Before going further east in Europe we might consider what was going on on the other side of the Atlantic. So long as the eastern states of America were English provinces, it was natural that their houses should be basically English in character. Throughout most of the eighteenth century they followed, perhaps a little tardily, the current Georgian idiom, in many cases adapted to wooden construction in place of brick and stone. Interiors tended to be simple, sometimes panelled, but enriched more by the fine furniture imported from England than by any elaborate architectural decoration.

During the second half of the century, American furniture of the best quality began to be made in places like Philadelphia (which long remained the cultural centre), Baltimore and Boston, and a recognisable American style with its own regional variations developed from the English prototypes.

The Crimson drawing-room, Carlton House, London. The architect, Henry Holland, began reconstructing Carlton House for the Prince of Wales as soon as it was made over to him on his majority in 1783. Work proceeded spasmodically under Holland's direction until 1805, when he was superseded by other nominees of the Prince. This view, from Pyne's Royal Residences, *shows the appearance of the room about 1819, furnished in the most lavish manner with magnificent draperies*

In the last years before 1800 and in those that followed, the principal architects working in the United States were still mainly British, but the new political and cultural affinities with France brought several distinguished practitioners from that country, encouraged by President Thomas Jefferson (1743–1826), a friend of Clérisseau though himself an architect in the English Palladian tradition. Among these were the architects Maximilian Godefroy (c. 1760–1833) and J.J. Remée (1764–1842) and the engineer P.C. L'Enfant (1754–1825) who laid out the plan for Washington DC during the 1790s.

Jefferson exercised great influence in the architectural development of the United States, at Washington and at Charlottesville where he built the University of Virginia. His work has a European sophistication that is perhaps best seen in Monticello, the charming domed and porticoed house he built for himself near Charlottesville.

In New York, John McComb designed the beautiful City Hall in 1803–12, with its curved staircase and fine rooms.

The British architects working in America at this time included James Hoban (1762–1831), an Irishman who designed the White House at Washington in the 1790s (it was restored by Latrobe after the war of 1812 and has undergone subsequent alteration); William Thornton (1759–1828), an English amateur who went to America in 1787 and, with his assistant George Hadfield (1764–1826), the designer of Arlington, and the French architect E. S. Hallet, built the original Capitol in 1793; and Benjamin Latrobe (1764–1820), a pupil of Samuel Pepys Cockerell.

On his arrival in 1796 Latrobe introduced to America from England and Germany the

highest architectural standards, and his ability was soon recognised by Thomas Jefferson who made him Surveyor of Public Buildings in 1803. He thereupon assumed control of the building of the Capitol and carried out its restoration after the fire of 1814. He resigned in 1817, when the work was taken over by the Bostonian Charles Bulfinch (1763–1844) who completed the central rotunda. The surviving early interiors are mostly Latrobe's work, including the semi-circular colonnaded House Chamber.

Although mainly associated with monumental Classic buildings, Latrobe also designed in Gothic, like most of his contemporaries. He left able pupils, including Robert Mills (1781–1855), Government Architect and Engineer from 1836 till 1851, who designed most of the great monumental buildings of the 1830s in Washington, as well as houses at Richmond, Virginia; and William Strickland (1788–1854) of Philadelphia.

Other Englishmen working in the eastern states were John Haviland (1792–1858), a cousin of Haydon the painter and a pupil of the architect James Elmes (1782–1862); and William Jay, designer of the Owens-Thomas House (1816) at Savannah, Georgia. At Charleston, South Carolina, are some earlier houses with handsome rooms, such as the Gabriel Manigault house, 1790–7.

Grand architecture in North America during this period is to be found mainly in its public and official buildings. With regard to domestic interiors, people were at that time more concerned with the realities of life than with display in their homes, and the emphasis was on elegance and comfort.

As well as those that remain in their original setting, many charming rooms that would otherwise have vanished are now preserved in museums.

Eastern Europe

Returning to Europe and moving further east, we find in the states of the Austro-Hungarian Empire many examples of the style that had currently become international, although we generally associate these lands more with the Baroque and Rococo of earlier generations. Most of the great Viennese palaces, for example, are Baroque and Rococo. But the Palais Klamm is Classic of the early nineteenth century and so is the Palais Rasumovsky, built in 1805–11 for Prince Rasumovsky, Russian Ambassador and patron of Beethoven.

This house has splendid interiors. A great circular hall with coffered dome leads into a noble ballroom of chamois and white scagliola, with a peristyle of Corinthian columns. From its ceiling hang five immense gilt chandeliers. The palace was designed by Louis Joseph von Montoyer (c. 1749–1811).

Meanwhile in Austria, as elsewhere in varying degrees, Gothic was adopted for romantic follies such as the charmingly absurd castle of Franzenburg at Laxemburg, near Vienna, as well as for works of a more serious nature. Amusing but even more absurd was the Central European fashion for rooms in which everything – chairs, tables, chandeliers and all – were made entirely of antlers, a fashion especially popular in Austria, as at Trautenfels in Styria.

The principal architects working in Vienna at this time, in addition to Montoyer, a Walloon, included Karl von Moreau (1758–1841), who was probably French, the Swiss Peter von Nobile (1774–1854) and, a little later, the Danish H. C. Hansen (1803–83) and his brother Theophil (1813–91). This shows the extent to which architecture had become international, for the Hansens were also employed in Greece.

In Greece, too, on the Island of Corfu, we find the work of an English architect, General Sir George Whitmore, R. E., in the royal palace built in 1819 which contains rooms of the utmost splendour in an Anglicised version of Empire.

While in Poland, a little earlier, between 1784 and 1793, the Italian Domenico Merlini reconstructed Lazienki for Stanislaus Augustus Poniatowski, the last King of Poland. Its large, white ballroom has a massive Classic simplicity, with Ionic pilasters, attic windows above the lower cornice and a diamond-coffered cove above the upper one. The Solomon Room is richer, with arches and Biblical paintings by Bacciarelli.

Russia

But it was in Russia that Classic interior design bore some of its richest fruit. Here, throughout the eighteenth century and into the nineteenth, current taste was determined mainly by that of successive sovereigns who, beginning with Peter the Great, enthusiastically adopted the changing fashions of the West and, with immense financial resources, plentiful labour and an abundance of rich materials, were able to give exceptionally free rein to their possibilities.

With the gold and the malachite, the lapis lazuli and porphyry and amber, the agate

Queen Luise's living-room
in the castle at Berlin.
Although decorated and given
its circular form in 1791 by
Langhans, this view shows
the room filled with early
nineteenth-century furniture
and gives a very fine picture
of the way such a room was
set out at this period

crystal and bronze and all the treasure from the Ural Mountains, combined with coloured glass and porcelain, western elegance was enriched with oriental splendour.

The early Classic Revival coincided with the reign of Catherine II, in whom it had no keener disciple. By 1779, in addition to the Russian architects who worked for her – Bazhenov, Starov and Matvei Feodorovich Kazakov – she had imported the Jacobite Scot, Charles Cameron (c. 1740–1812), then living in Rome and, soon afterwards, the Italian Giacomo Quarenghi (1744–1817). These two became her favourite architects.

Cameron introduced to Russia the style made popular by his compatriot Robert Adam, but developed it in a highly individual manner. At Tsarskoye Seloe the green walls of his dining room are decorated with almost life-size figures in white bas-relief, by the Ukrainian sculptor Martos, amid Pompeiian plaster arabesques; while Catherine's bedroom is adorned with clusters of slender, free-standing porcelain columns and Wedgwood plaques – an entirely Pompeiian design. Both these rooms, as in most of the Russian palaces, have finely inlaid parquet floors. Both have recently been almost miraculously restored after devastation in World War II, as the 'Chambres d'Agate' in Tsarkoye Seloe soon will be.

Between 1781 and 1796, on Catherine's instructions, Cameron was building the palace of Pavlovsk for her son Paul. Here are some of the best interiors of the period. From a rusticated entrance hall, Egyptian in character, an enclosed staircase leads to the *piano nobile* where we find Cameron's round and lofty upper hall with mauve and white scagliola walls and large niches, with a recessed gallery and caryatids above.

Cameron, however, did not get on well with Paul, who dropped him after Catherine's death in 1796, and Pavlovsk was finished by his pupil Vicenzo Brenna, Quarenghi and others. Quarenghi's work is more akin to that of contemporary France – richer in sculpture and painting than Cameron's but neither so elegant nor so original. He was kept on by Paul but discarded by Alexander who succeeded Paul in 1801.

There is about many of the Russian interiors of this period, notwithstanding their considerable grandeur, a kind of rational unpretentiousness which adds much to their charm. A great deal of the decoration of ceilings and walls is done in flat, painted *grisaille*, resembling raised plasterwork but more restful to the eye. Upper floors, if they contain only rooms of minor importance, are approached by light wooden side staircases rather than those often seen in English houses of the same period, which dominate the house and are far too grand for the ordinary rooms to which they lead. These qualities can be seen in such houses as Archangelskoye near Moscow.

Meanwhile in Russia may be found greater variety in the shapes of rooms – by means of screens, apses and recesses – than perhaps in any other country.

On his succession, Alexander I reinstated Cameron, then sixty-one, but his chief architects were the Frenchman Thomas de Thomon (1754–1813) and the Russians Andrei Nikiforovich Voronikhin (1760–1814) and Adrian Dimitrievich Zakharov (1761–1811). Their successors in the triumphant years following the defeat of Napoleon were Vasili Petrovich Stasov (1769–1848), Alphonse Montferrand, a pupil of Percier and Fontaine, and designer of the rather uninspired St Isaac's Cathedral in St Petersburg; and

ROMANTIC REVIVAL

Brenna's talented pupil, Karl Ivanovich Rossi (1775–1844), born of a Russian father and an Italian ballerina.

Rossi, an able planner, was the 'John Nash' of Petersburg, designing many of its finest streets and squares. In 1812, on the *Ile de Pierre* he built the palace of Yelagin for the Tsar, containing much characteristically Russian *grisaille* painting and gilded maple-wood doors. Designs for some of the interiors made at the time by the decorator Scotti were never carried out until recently, from the original drawings, as part of the great restorations currently in progress.

In 1819 Scotti, one of a large family, was again working with Rossi in the fine interiors of the great palace in Petersburg designed by Rossi for the Grand Duke Michael, since 1890 the Russian Museum. Once more we find rich, flat-painted and gilt ceilings, and gilded sycamore or maple-wood doors. There is a great white and gold pillared hall with magnificent gold furniture by Rossi.

Alexander was succeeded on his death in 1825 by Nicholas I, during whose reign, which ended in 1855, the rather insensitive Montferrand continued to work on St Isaac's Cathedral, completed in 1858, while the New Hermitage was built from designs by Leo von Klenze of Munich, carried out by Stasov and Yepinov.

These huge interiors, dating from the late 1830s, are of fine quality but lack the freshness of Klenze's work in Munich. They belong to the closing stages of the Classical revival.

opposite. *The dining room at 13 Lincoln's Inn Fields, London, in the house built for himself by the architect Sir John Soane in 1813*

opposite. *Ante-room to the royal bedroom, Palace of Caserta, near Naples, Italy. The vocabulary of Romantic Classicism is by this time becoming inflated into forms that are much more associated with High Victorian than Late Empire*

Haga Slot, Stockholm

The interior of this little castle was completed about 1790 and the charming divan room spans interestingly the styles of the eighteenth and nineteenth centuries

Seabrooke House, near Charleston, South Carolina, USA

The entrance hall and dining room: this grand and formal interior gives a clear picture of the tastes of the plantation owners in the southern states. The house was completed about 1810

above. *Hall at Wilanów, near Warsaw, Poland. The castle was originally built for King John Sobieski between 1624 and 1696, and various additions were made in the mid-eighteenth century. A considerable amount of redecoration was done in the early nineteenth century, and the hall dates from this period. Yellow Sienna marble columns, marble panels and grisaille trompe-l'oeil paintings are all combined in a sophisticated manner to produce a scheme of considerable interest*

above. *The library, Abbey of Klosterneuburg, near Vienna, Austria. Of all the abbey libraries in Southern Germany and Austria this one is unique in that it was decorated in the early nineteenth century. It was built to designs of Joseph Kornhäusel between 1836–42 and is, excluding churches, possibly the largest Romantic Classical interior in existence*

Pavlovsk Palace, near Leningrad, Russia

left. The lantern study, built by Charles Cameron for the Grand Duke Paul and Grand Duchess Marie Feodorovna between 1781 and 1796. It is uncertain how much of this large building is attributable to that strange Scottish emigré, but this room bears the stamp of his developed later style

below. The picture gallery at Pavlovsk Palace. This gallery was designed by V. Brenna, an Italian architect who was Cameron's collaborator and eventual successor on this project

Château de Malmaison, near Paris

Josephine's bedroom: redecorated in 1810 for the Empress Josephine by Percier and Fontaine, it is filled with magnificent furniture of the period, signed by Jacob Desmalter and Biennais

National Theatre, Munich, Germany

The foyer. Originally built by Karl von Fischer in 1811–18, the theatre was burned down in 1823 and rebuilt in its original form by von Klenze. The interior has recently been beautifully restored once again after war damage

Apsley House, London

The Waterloo Gallery: intended specifically to accommodate the annual Waterloo banquet, this great room was
added on to the existing house for the first Duke of Wellington in 1829. The architect was Benjamin Dean Wyatt

opposite. Part of one of the table services presented to the first Duke of Wellington

Royal Palace of Caserta, Naples, Italy

left. *A bedroom, showing a very late but very full-blooded expression of the Empire style*

below. *A bathroom. Another very late flowering of the Empire style. The bath is based on Roman precedent and the alabaster dressing table has a fountain for perfume in the centre*

Castello di Raconigi, near Turin, Italy

opposite. *Decorated panel on one of the doors of the Etruscan room, Castello di Raconigi, near Turin, Italy, dating from 1834*

Palazzo Ducale, Mantua, Italy

opposite. The bedroom which was decorated in the Empire style by Guiseppe Piermarini and used in 1812 by Eugène Beauharnais

Royal Palace, Turin, Italy

A detail of the very rich carving on one of the window linings in the council chamber. It was designed by Pelagio Palagi for King Carlo Alberto in 1840, and the carvers were Capello, Ferrero and Marielloni

HIGH VICTORIAN 1840-80

Denys Hinton

The Most High and Mighty Princess Alexandrina Victoria, Queen of Great Britain and Ireland and Empress of India, lent her name to a variety of things, among them a London railway station, an outsize water lily, a military decoration for valour, countless theatres, a private carriage and the largest lake in Africa. Above all, we associate the name with a moral attitude and a distinctive mode of decoration: the one disciplined and puritanical; the other, paradoxically, licentious and undiscriminating. This feat of identification is all the more astonishing when one reflects that it applied not only to Britain or indeed to her Empire, but to America and large sections of Europe; and all the more confusing because, in the international sense, Victorian standards are seen against the background which is also a compound of conflicting elements. The careless optimism of the western pioneers or the moral rectitude and hypocrisy of the English middle class; the tired cynicism of the French intellectual set against the naive idealism of the Italian freedom fighter.

It is particularly ironical that the generic term 'Victorian' should originate with an English monarch whose influence in matters of artistic fashion was small; nevertheless each of us conjures up his own clear mind-picture when the word is mentioned.

To Thomas Harris when he first used the phrase 'Victorian architecture' in 1860, it meant a self-conscious and strident style of his own invention: a style which, fortunately, did not earn widespread adoption, despite an earnest desire of many designers of the day to create a novel, contemporary and indigenous visual language.

We can now see that Harris was writing during what we call the 'high phase' of Victorian taste. To understand the significance of this, we have to adopt a favourite theory of the Victorians themselves, that any artistic style develops from a faltering 'adolsecence' to a high point of mature achievement and then on to a period of obsolescence and decay which allows another, more virile mode to supersede it. In this survey it will be convenient to date the High Victorian phase between the year 1840 and the early 1880s when, to quote a writer in the *Architectural Review*:

The application of electric power to the lighting of streets and buildings became practical: conversation over long distances by telephone a reality; chilled meat a dietary and anything in the revised Queen Anne style the rage.

opposite. Drawing room from a house in Savannah, Georgia, USA. Built in the first half of the nineteenth century, this room is typical of the standard domestic interior of this period. The mouldings gradually fattened and the details became bolder as the century advanced

HIGH VICTORIAN

Some critics narrow down this period to the twenty years which followed the International 1851 Exhibition in London, and much that follows in this account can well be illustrated within these narrower limits.

If Victorian life inherited much from its predecessors, it is still true that important new developments gave to nineteenth-century buildings, and their interiors, a uniquely novel character, so that they cannot be mistaken for examples of any earlier period, even when they were trying hard to imitate them. Perhaps the most significant of these developments was the rapid increase in specialisation, resulting from a steady rise in standards of living. This was true not only of the individual dwelling, with more and more rooms set aside for occasional special uses, but also of the creation of a new class of specialised buildings for leisure and instruction. Opera houses began to appear in small capitals and provincial centres: even in isolated rubber settlements in the Amazon basin, and public concert halls followed suit. The spa habit received a tremendous boost from the over-indulgence common to the *nouveaux riches* and the older aristocracy, while the casino offered its own attractions to those taking the waters. Around the casino and the turf revolved much of the smartest social activity of the time.

What was true of 'society' began to be true even of the skilled artisan class, for whom the railway boom of the 1840s had made possible a visit to one of the new seaside resorts. The unequal standards of the coaching inn gave way rapidly to the new catering provisions of the railway age: provisions which themselves ranged widely from the opulence of the aristocratic hotels and restaurants on the one hand to the apartments of the seaside landlady on the other.

To the Victorians of the English-speaking world, leisure meant uplift, useful knowledge and improving books, showing a zeal for self-improvement exercised nowadays more widely in the Soviet Union, Japan and the emerging nations than in western Europe. The museum, art gallery and public library seem in retrospect to typify better than any other type of building the aspirations of this High Victorian generation. A good second in this respect come the administrative buildings.

An ever-widening franchise and the spread of Parliamentary ideas throughout Europe after 1848 produced not only the legislators' headquarters, the Reichstag and the Parliament House of Budapest among them, but also a remarkable range of civic buildings combining administrative quarters with ambitious reception suites. It is easy to see why successful solutions of this difficult and complex problem, such as Waterhouse's Town Hall at Manchester, attracted widespread attention and were imitated freely.

Standards, as has been said, were rising throughout Europe and America, although not everywhere at the same rate. The 1851 Exhibition catalogue stated:

. . . in the United States, it is rare to find wealth so accumulated as to favour the expenditure of large sums upon articles of luxury.

Yet before the end of the century the American millionaire had stamped his influence on the decorative styles of Europe and the USA and had infiltrated the highest circles in the older societies. European and American millionaires were, however, outstandingly

opposite. *The cedar stair, Harlaxton Manor, Lincolnshire, England. An extraordinary* tour-de-force, *elaborate even for Victorian England. The architect was William Burn, and the date about 1855. Except for the fragrant cedar woodwork of the stair and doorways, all the remainder of the decoration is carried out in plaster, even the cords and tassels which swing slightly at the touch*

conservative in their tastes and their patronage served to consolidate prevailing fashions.

The word 'luxury' in the quotation is the key to mid-Victorian attitudes, having undergone a subtle change of emphasis since the days when *luxuria* implied sexual indulgence. In their homes and public rooms the Victorians developed an obsession with luxurious comfort, or rather the *appearance* of comfort, since very few of the furniture designs, for instance, were scientifically adapted to the needs of the human body at rest. This appearance of comfort applied even when in transit, specifically in the railway train (Pullman sleeping cars date from the late 60s) and on board ship. As the years pass, the saloons and state rooms of steamships abandon the honest 'ship-shape' character of the early Mississippi paddle steamers, with their exposed wooden framework, and take on the padding and ornament of landlubbers' quarters, striving, it seems, to persuade the passengers that they have never left the shore.

The royal quarters on the *Victoria and Albert*, launched in 1854, although wallpapered and upholstered in a floral chintz design, retain much of the freshness which land-based rooms had lost by that date. The LNW Railway royal carriage, however, was not commissioned until 1869 and its quilted silk ceiling and upholstery, its fringed curtains and its patterned carpet all echo the prevailing opulence of the day, without escaping altogether the character of a padded cell.

Comfort to the Victorians meant more than well-padded furniture. They expected rooms which were adequately heated, lit and drained, but above all they were obsessed with the benefits of ventilation. Chadwick's public health reports at least persuaded the English middle classes to attend to the hygiene of their own homes, if not to improve those of their workers. In an age still largely ignorant of micro-biology, cross ventilation was expected to work the necessary miracles (even sufferers from pulmonary tuberculosis were for the first time exposed to fresh air!). The results were higher rooms fitted with large plate-glass sash windows. Top-lit staircase halls gave access to bedrooms and helped to eliminate dark and draughty corridors. As early as 1814 Benjamin Wyatt recommended this arrangement to the Duke of Wellington because:

. . . in this way I could produce an effect which should be so striking that the impression made upon the Spectator, upon his first entrance, should afterwards be kept up by a moderate degree of space and enrichment in the rest of the Building.

The central, multi-storied hall was in time to become a principal living space of the house but until the reintroduction of central heating, first in America, then in Europe, draughts needed control – by folding screens, strategically placed and by heavy hangings across doors and windows. Privacy was secured and glare eliminated by draping or stretching lace curtains inside the glass and by fitting pitch-pine Venetian shutters.

The advent of the incandescent gas mantle late in the century converted artificial lighting from a dim, smelly, spluttering inconvenience into something capable of enhancing a decorative scheme by allowing it, for the first time, to be seen as a whole. Before this date we need to visualise the Victorian interior after nightfall as a series of narrow rings of light amid prevailing gloom. The dark unreflective surfaces of walls and ceiling did serve,

opposite. The Library at the Reform Club, London. Completed in 1840 and probably the masterwork of Sir Charles Barry, this interior shows Victorian architecture at its most impressive

however, to ensure that working surfaces (the table or the needlework stool) were more brightly lit than their surroundings. A modern billiards room suggests the atmosphere which must have prevailed throughout the Victorian house.

In already industrialised societies the dominant group was a rising middle class who, as stock- or shareholders were rivals to the traditional landed interests and were distrusted by them on this score. What needs to be emphasised is that this middle class, far from wishing to promote distinctly *bourgeois* standards, devoted itself to imitating the manners and fashions of the older aristocracies.

The defence of the upper classes lay in erecting a wall of protocol and convention to deter all but the most adaptable of the *parvenues*. French, British and German protocol may differ in emphasis but is alike in intention. Those who failed to surmount this obstacle to social acceptance were satirised in *Punch* in the character of Sir Gorgius Midas and in Trollope's railway contractor, Roger Scatchard, whose 'show rooms of Boxall Hill were furnished most magnificently but they were set apart for company; and as the company never came – seeing that they were never invited – the grand rooms and the grand furniture were not of much material use to Lady Scatchard'. The intricacies of Victorian etiquette served to fill some of the time which lay heavy on the hands of the middle-class housewife, while in the larger household, the planning of entertainment and the management of an army of servants not only occupied the attention but demanded space and furniture far beyond that required for family living. The head of the household saw his part in all this as the provision of employment for members of the lower orders.

English political life revolved, to an extent unknown today, around the country house

Perspective view of the entrance hall at Sandringham, Norfolk, drawn by E. C. Sayer in 1870. The wainscot, door and window linings and carved work in the screen and ceiling would be in oak or walnut with a natural finish, heightened by other woods in contrasting bands. The flat portions of the walls would be covered in a dark self-pattern paper, sometimes imitating Spanish leather

week-end party and the political dinner party in town: Stafford House and Devonshire House, for instance, in their scale and opulence, certainly reflect the status of those who met there and the importance of the decisions they reached. In humbler homes everywhere was carried on a complex ritual of 'at-homes', involving the leaving and returning of *cartes de visite*: a pale reflection of the royal presentation parties or 'drawing rooms' around which, until recently, the London season revolved.

This rigidity of social structure left little scope for originality of ideas in decoration or furnishing. The aesthetic movement of the 1880s took root, significantly, amongst a radical and slightly eccentric coterie, well outside the accepted social circles, and was ridiculed by W. S. Gilbert and the *Punch* cartoonists. Originality was discouraged in another respect by the rise of manufacturing processes. Firms such as John G. Crace and Hardman, with whom Pugin collaborated, Cremer or Lemoine in Paris or Martinotti in Turin, who appeared in the 1862 Exhibition, or William Watt, for whom Godwin supplied designs, were all representative of the new economic organisation. A vast increase in demand led naturally to repetitive production of furniture, fabrics and decorative objects generally without, as yet, entirely eliminating the unique set piece, the price of which, nevertheless, rose disproportionately. It was no accident that William Morris, in order to promote his own very different aims and compete for commissions, should have set up a commercial company in 1861.

Victorians were sufficiently intrigued by the ingenuity of new processes and materials to ignore the dangers of a situation in which, as Gottfried Semper put it, 'means and materials of production have outrun artistic invention'. It was common to find new

HIGH VICTORIAN

materials or techniques imitating the traditional, and this was received with pride and satisfaction rather than any sense of shame or incongruity.

The results of such enthusiasms were clearly seen in the 1851 Exhibition. Prince Albert's vague dissatisfaction with the standards of the manufactured 'art-objects' was shared by others of the organisers, especially Sir Henry Cole, who devoted his energies in the following years to 'connecting the best Art with familiar objects in daily use'. It can have given him little encouragement to find Ruskin sustaining the myth of a hierarchy of art, with the fine arts, especially painting, at one level, through which alone truly artistic sentiments could be expressed, contrasted with forms of inferior art 'such as will be by their simplicity less liable to injury . . .'

Whatever the standards reached by the objects which were scattered around the Victorian home, it could not be denied that there were many more of them than ever before. At no period before or since have movable objects played so vital a part in deciding the character of an interior as they did in mid-Victorian Europe.

Their bewildering variety and their apparently random arrangement are meaningless to us, but to their owner they formed collectively a museum of his or her personal life, *not* of his or her artistic taste (most of the articles were collected and arranged by women, with a place for everything and everything in its place). A comparatively small number of Victorian householders collected antique pieces, generally heavy Jacobean furniture items, but the fondness for the antique, together with the collecting habit and a certain eclectic taste were all inherited by the Victorians from their Romantic predecessors. (In 1890 'a touch of eclecticism' was considered 'always so agreeable in a thoroughly-studied drawing room'.)

Most householders filled their rooms with mementos – presents from friends or emigrant relatives, who contributed 'native craft-work' items, souvenirs of holidays specially manufactured for tourists (wood-carving from Oberammergau and the like), samplers embroidered by the girls of the family, religious texts and, of course, the ubiquitous photographs: school, college and wedding groups and studio portraits by the dozen. All classes of society were affected by the mania, royalty conspicuous among them.

What are we to make of these personal museums? On the one hand they seem to fulfil an almost universal desire for individual expression or, more accurately, the expression of each family's relations with an outside world which was becoming increasingly impersonal. At its worst, however, the obsession with mementos takes on the overtones of a fetish, or at least extends the Victorians' characteristic sentimentality to quite unhealthy lengths. Two examples come to mind, one fictional, the other fact. Dickens wrote of Miss Havisham in *Great Expectations* sitting in a darkened room surrounded by the mouldering ruins of a gargantuan wedding breakfast, laid out on that morning when she was jilted at the church door. This was written in 1860, and a year later nature almost imitated art when Queen Victoria, on Albert's death, insisted on retaining all his rooms identically as he had used them and began to sleep with a wreath above the bed where her dead husband had lain. In both these all too characteristic examples the objects in the case are not only reminders, they have become substitutes for experience.

Pressing the museum analogy, we find certain sections devoted to the interests of the man; others exclusively to his wife's. The head of the household at home in his smoking room or away at his club, working in his study or relaxing in his private billiards room or over the brandy after dinner, was secure in an exclusively masculine world, and his environment reflected this atmosphere: cosy but a little severe, the walls in all probability panelled and the furniture upholstered in leather and quilted with what Praz in his *History of Interior Decoration* calls 'navel-like buttons', reminding us that the belly is the anatomical region *bourgeois par excellence*. On the walls hung hunting trophies under glass, perhaps as proof against moths, or at least there was a steel engraving of the 'Stag at Bay' in lieu. In the male rooms there would have been as few hangings as possible to allay the Victorian ladies' horror of stale cigar smoke. Ash trays and spittoons would be in evidence.

The drawing room, on the other hand, was the core of a suite of rooms over which the lady of the house presided, well described as 'the domestic shrine of beauty and refinement'. The largest houses could boast, in addition, a ballroom or gallery and a music room while, opening out from many drawing rooms, in northern Europe at least, was a conservatory – the bad-weather substitute for the Mediterranean terrace or the open-sided verandah so typical of American houses of this period. Thomas Hopper's Gothic iron and glass conservatory at Carlton House in London was made as early as 1807, but the Crystal Palace was probably responsible for the widespread popularity of the conservatory in England. It was an ideal, and became the traditional place to propose marriage. Miniature greenhouses or Wardian chambers were also built into the windows of the period.

Plants which needed less light were freely admitted into the drawing room itself, some-times to excess as in the Château de Saint Gratien in the 1860s. Potted bourbon palms and the aspidistra have adapted themselves best to the ecology of the European drawing room.

The drawing room itself in many nineteenth-century houses had descended from the *piano nobile* to a somewhat raised ground floor. Significantly, it had taken the place of the boudoir of the *ancien régime* as the lady's reception room. It might be of more than one cell, linked by a draped archway or a tripartite openwork screen, and was often *en suite* with the dining room through folding doors or a screen. It was, of course, profusely furnished, chiefly with pieces for sitting on. A contemporary account of the drawing room at Sandringham will amplify the details:

We are looking into a room which is lived in: which is impressed with a personality, and such signs of individuality make *the true value of decoration* [my italics]. The charm is not easy to define. It does not arise only from the books and music here and there, the embroidery or sketches, the feather screens or painted china which discover the lady's skill and taste: it is rather in the whole atmosphere, the colours and the arrangement that the subtle influence reveals itself.

The scheme of colour in this room is characteristically beautiful. The furniture is up-holstered in light blue with just some threads of crimson and gold; light blue is the pre-dominant colour of the panelling; a rose tint gives a dainty flush to the walls and the mouldings are cream and gold. Despite any fashion of terra-cotta or canary, the one colour for a drawing-room must always remain blue; it is bright and sunny in the daytime and very becoming and brilliant when lighted in the evening.

A certain richness is added to this elegance by hangings of chenille and Indian rugs on the polished oak floor. The most remarkable ornament in the room is of the Princess's [Alexandra of Wales] own designing – a rockery grown with ferns and exquisite roses, from which rises a figure of Venus. Among the palms in the conservatory is a group of bathing nymphs by Mme Jérichau.

This was a drawing room built and assembled shortly after 1870 – earlier rooms had presented a rather more sombre air, with very dark, rather over-polished furniture and a good deal of crimson in the hangings and glass ornaments betraying, says Praz, the prevailing romantic emotionalism.

There was ample scope for eccentric schemes of decoration such as the tartan suite at Balmoral: an idea which appears again in the royal palace at Dresden. Tartan decoration, in a Scottish mansion, acted as an easily recognised though rather oblique symbol. Victorian symbolism was generally far more precise and, since it played a major part in the visual environment, it deserves mention here. To the Victorians 'every picture told a story', and since in the main there was a lack of understanding of the classical symbolic language, the stories had to be simple ones with which the owners could identify themselves, and visual platitudes abounded.

Of the narrative schools of painting, the historical school, associated with the names of Haydon in England and Overbeck and Cornelius in Germany, is perhaps best represented by the monumental frescoes in the Palace of Westminster, although most town halls featured something of the kind. There was nothing essentially new about the *genre*: think

of Laguerre's Blenheim paintings at Marlborough House, London, for instance.

On the other hand, the anecdotal school of Frith and Augustus Egg, and their manner, produced mainly for the walls of the drawing room, remained popular in certain academic art circles until very recent years. Pre-Raphaelite work such as the Briar Rose series at Buscot Park falls into this category of narrative, although presented in a rather specialised poetic language.

Narrative subjects, however, were not content to remain within the picture frame. They began to appear in low-relief plaster around the deep friezes which became fashionable in the 70s, suggesting the Hardwick Hall Great Chamber which, being an Elizabethan work, was thought in acceptable taste. Narrative also appeared on furniture, carved in very high relief in limewood or Irish bog oak; qualifying, in a phrase of 1851, as 'intellectual ornamentation'. The technique and the sentiment alike owed much to German influence. So important, indeed, did this narrative aspect become, that classical standards of proportion, scale and integrity were not so much flouted as ignored altogether.

Richard Redgrave RA, in a report published by the Great Exhibition juries in 1852, praised a highly overworked mammoth walnut sideboard by Fourdinois as:

. . . an apt illustration of ornament having a just and characteristic significance and fitted for the purpose for which it is intended. Six dogs, emblematical of the chase . . . are not merely imitative but are treated as part of an ornamental bracket or console, thus composed architecturally for bearing support. Standing on four pedestals are female figures gracefully

HIGH VICTORIAN

designed as emblems of the four quarters of the world, bearing the most useful production of their climate as contributions to the feast.

This is a very early attempt to influence taste within the pages of a semi-official report: a trend which was to develop in the second half of the century, along with the award of medals and trophies to chosen designs. It is impossible to exaggerate the importance of the machinery of international exhibitions in spreading ideas, both technological and aesthetic, in a way in which the travels of the English aristocrat once had done.

France was long familiar with the idea of a purely *national* exhibition of manufactures when the British, at Hyde Park in 1851, extended the idea to a world-wide scale. But this was merely the beginning of the story, and events in London in 1862 and in Paris in 1855, 1867 and 1878 consolidated the progress made in exchanging ideas and experience. The Philadelphia Centennial Exhibition of 1876 performed a like service for the USA, widening her familiarity with European fashions and recognising, in return, the contribution she was then beginning to make. Leadership in matters of taste was certainly needed: Wayne Andrews, writing specifically of the USA, calls the years during and after the Civil War 'The Age of Indecision' – and this uncertainty was not confined to the States!

Stylistic change in the High Victorian years proceeded erratically but was, nonetheless, considerable. In the remaining pages of this section one can only touch on a few significant turning points, at times deliberately simplifying a notoriously complex subject. The modern critic may need, in fact, to disregard as far as he can the several modes of 'fancy dress' adopted by the Victorians in order to trace the essentially nineteenth-century character underneath.

What, firstly, have these modes of fancy dress in common? Like the earlier designs of the Romantics they are to a degree associational, reminding one of some literary or historical attribute. They have shed some of the naivety (and the charm) of the early Romantics and have become at once more earnest and more adventurous in combining their motifs.

There was a mainstream of taste which we might call the opulent mode and which its creators called 'a free treatment of the Renaissance style', and a minority taste developed alongside on very different lines: concerned more with the alien, the exotic or the consciously aesthetic elements, and for a short time in England and parts of Germany this specialised taste was openly and exclusively Gothic. The minority included the nineteenth-century names such as William Morris which are most respected today but which their contemporaries regarded with some distrust. We owe to their adventurous spirit and lack of complacency any progress which may since have been made. First, however, examine the mainstream of 'smart' taste and we shall discover how persistent was the attraction of this mixed Franco-Italian Renaissance style, from the 1820s through to the years of Edward VII, and how widespread its appeal throughout Europe and America.

Insofar as one can generalise, the Italian *cinquecento* tradition provided the architectural skeleton and the *Louis Quatorze* or *Louis Quinze* styles the decoration and the furniture. Interiors which incorporated loggias or galleries: Osborne or Ferriers or Barry's London clubs, have come to be regarded as Italian in inspiration: others, like Benjamin Wyatt's Stafford House, or his cousin Jeffrey's reception rooms at Windsor, are wholeheartedly

opposite. *The Salon in the Château de Ferrières, Seine et Marne, France. Rich, upholstered, impressive yet comfortable, the building was designed for Baron James de Rothschild by Paxton and the decoration of the interior was completed by the early 1860s to designs by the painter Eugène Lami*

French. These are early examples and, properly speaking, fall outside our period, but the idea was taken up in the Great Western Hotel in London and in the Shiff house in America during the years 1849–51. What is remarkable about all these early instances of what came to be known as the *Impératrice* or Second Empire style, is that they were developed outside France and pre-date the establishment of Louis Napoleon's Empire in 1852.

Paris was recognised as the source of fashion and Britain's dependence on foreign, and especially French, designs was strengthened by the patent and copyright position. Printed textile designs before 1839, and designs for other manufactured items after that date, were protected by patent legislation: the immediate effect was widespread pirating of foreign designs by British manufacturers, notably Manchester calico printers and Birmingham brass and bronze workers.

It was to be expected that French Imperial patronage, and specifically the Louvre extensions and the Paris Opera, should have given a strong impetus to the Second Empire manner throughout the capitals of Europe. (Much of the Whitehall rebuilding proposals and the Vienna Ringstrasse were in direct emulation.) As we have seen, Napoleon III's support for international exhibitions ensured the rapid spread of Parisian innovations.

An immediate effect was the appearance in the drawing- and dining-rooms of Europe of a selection of huge sideboards, cabinets and *étagères*, which may have been in scale with the exhibition halls in which they were first displayed but were not in scale with any but the largest houses. Morris called this 'state furniture' and justified his own designs in the *genre* 'as much for beauty's sake as for use'. The 1851 jury, on the other hand, voiced 'one legitimate regret that, amidst all the ornamental works in furniture collected at the exhibition, there were to be found so few specimens of ordinary furniture for general use'. The tables and cabinets in *boulle* work – ebonised hardwood with inlay of ivory, mother of pearl, tortoise-shell or ormolu – are indeed not without appeal: in the search for Victorian 'antiques' one foresees their eventual appearance in the international salerooms.

Despite the facilities of repetitive production, such pieces were by their nature suited only to the pockets of rich men: the furniture trade regarded 'the French as a costly style and difficult to work'. That its popularity outlived the span of the Second Empire was largely due, as has been suggested above, to its adoption by the millionaires: specifically by the Rothschilds in Europe and the United Kingdom during the 1870s and 80s and by the Vanderbilts in Newport, Rhode Island, USA, in the following decade. Even as late as 1903 the Wehrner re-shaping of Luton Hoo was wholly French – more scholarly perhaps than its predecessors, but well within an accepted tradition.

For those who can take it, the exuberance of the Second Empire style is its redeeming characteristic, excusing the coarseness and hard linear quality of much of the decoration and justifying the almost complete disappearance of the plane surface, which in earlier periods had offered a little rest to the eye and allowed the more concentrated ornament its proper weight in the total decorative scheme.

In mid-century taste, the beautiful meant the intricately-ornamented. If we look back to seek the origin of this quaint notion, we shall find an echo in Burke's essay on 'The Sublime and the Beautiful', where beauty is made dependent on 'smallness, intricacy'

opposite. *The library and the gallery, Château de Grosbois, France. Originally built in 1580, the house was extensively altered by Napoleon's Maréchal Berthier in 1804, who built the miniature 'Galerie des Batailles' which can be seen through the opening. The library, reached from the gallery down a few steps, dates from later in the century and is correspondingly richer in treatment*

and even 'a moderate appearance of ill-health'. Not a bad recipe for Victorian taste!

The passion for enriching the enclosing surfaces of a room was by no means confined to those advocating or practising a 'free Renaissance' style. If we return to the opening of our chosen period, we shall find Pugin, the leading medievalist, pouring ornament, architectural and sculptural, over every available inch of space in the Palace of Westminster and his other secular works such as Scarisbrick Hall, thus creating an effect 'dark and solemn, for the display of the taste and art of dead men', as the 1851 organisers wrote of his medieval court at the Great Exhibition. Which was a little unfair to Pugin, who was in this respect only pressing one stage further a current popular taste for the medieval baronial life. (The prescribed styles for the Palace of Westminster competition entries were the Gothic or the Elizabethan.)

At a time when the first Reform Act was stripping the reality of political power from the English landed gentry, a sentimental longing for the trappings of manorial privilege was taking its place. Since the movement had passed its peak when Victoria came to the throne, this is not the place to dwell on the spate of 'manor houses' which were remodelled or new-built under the influence of these longings, except to say that their plans bore no relation to their acknowledged prototypes. It is true, nonetheless, that for many of the Englishmen of Victoria's reign who could afford to realise their ambitions, the manor house, with its aura of paternalistic dignity, remained a *beau idéal* of civilised living.

There was an element of fantasy inherent in this situation, which from time to time erupted in building activity so bizarre as to defy description. The best known examples internationally were the *Ludwigsschlösser*, particularly the fairy palace of Linderhof and the Wagnerian nightmare of Neuschwanstein, which were being built, on and off, throughout the 70s and 80s. They borrowed, perhaps unconsciously, from the English castle-building boom of the early years of the century: buildings of the class of Belvoir, Penrhyn and Harlaxton. All are charged with a heavy atmosphere of the imaginary past so intense as to seem claustrophobic. This is true also of William Burges's castles for the Marquess of Bute at Cardiff, built out of their time in the 60s and 70s, with more than a tinge of eastern splendour among the Gothic exuberance of the decoration.

Occasional Islamic designs, taking their clue from Sezincote, also appeared unexpectedly in the English countryside, as at Elveden in Suffolk where the style was chosen, rather tactlessly, for a Sikh Maharajah.

With architecture and decoration in this fevered state, it is a relief to find a few influential spokesmen advocating a breath of fresh country air, to lower the aesthetic temperature and so secure the survival and recovery of taste. In this task John Ruskin's influence was paramount, although few men have been so misunderstood by their disciples. One of his central and recurring themes was the dependence of art on natural forms, found in his writing, his drawings and his occasional excursions into decorative design, such as can be seen at Wallington in Northumberland, executed in 1855.

His botanical forms are obviously studied more closely and lovingly than those of his contemporaries, and they have been disciplined to suit two-dimensional technique in a way which Pugin advocated in his *Floriated Ornament* six years before: the effect resembles

The Music Room *by James McNeill Whistler. Painted in 1860, this charming picture evokes a quintessential period character*

the albums of pressed flowers which were popular at the time. 'Ancient artists', wrote Pugin, 'disposed the leaves and flowers of which their design was composed so as to *fill up* the space they were intended to enrich: for instance, a panel which by its very construction is flat would be ornamented by leaves or flowers drawn out or extended so as to display their geometric forms on a flat surface.' He goes on to contrast this heraldic approach with the work of his contemporaries who 'would endeavour to give a fictitious idea of relief, as if *bunches* of flowers were laid on'. It commends Pugin's persuasive powers that this principle was taken up in design schools of all kinds in the years which followed. We shall find that this, and similar ideas, anticipate and influence the textiles and wallpapers of Morris and the Arts and Crafts men, whose chief work enriches the late Victorian years.

Parallel movements in furniture design enabled an aesthetically-minded minority to present decorative schemes radically different from their more conservative neighbours. These differences must have seemed revolutionary at the time and they are typified for us by Philip Webb's Red House, built for Morris in 1859. C. L. Eastlake, Jnr, in 1868, published a book of designs entitled *Hints on Household Taste*: his examples were remarkable in three respects. The colour proposed for the furniture items was much nearer that of natural untreated wood than was currently approved; a beeswax finish was recommended in place of the french polishers' shellac and, more fundamentally, the construction of the pieces employed joinery rather than cabinet-making technique, with a minimum of three-dimensional mouldings. The net result was in a decidedly rustic taste and perhaps it is not surprising that Eastlake's ideas were more readily accepted in

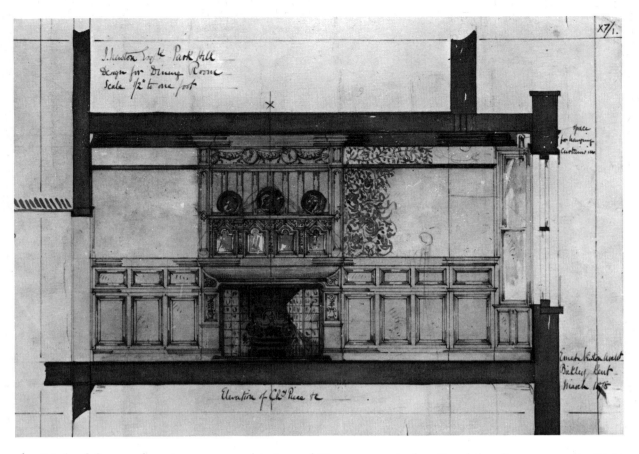

Drawing of the chimney-piece for the dining room at Park Hill, Croydon, England, by Ernest Newton, 1878. Certain elements of the characteristic style of the end of the century are very evident in this drawing – the coloured tiles, the wallpaper of the type associated with Morris, Crane or Shand Kydd, and finally the breakaway from Classical precedent in the forms of the chimney-piece, overmantel and panelling

the United States than in more sophisticated European circles. Eastlake disapproved of his medievalist colleagues Burges and Seddon when they applied oil-painted decoration to their furniture designs (both men exhibited pieces of this kind in 1862, as did Morris and Company) but the simpler shapes which became necessary when the pre-Raphaelites took to painting furniture advanced the trend towards plane surfaces which Eastlake himself had advocated.

Perhaps the most startling innovation was an importation from a source which for the previous fifty years had sealed itself hermetically from western influence – the empire of Japan. The romantic circumstances of Japan's 'opening' in the 1850s and the alien character of its civilisation captured the Victorian imagination, but Westerners' patronising approach prevented a serious attempt to understand or interpret that civilisation. The result in artistic terms repeated the story of *chinoiserie* a century before. An imperfectly understood hotch-potch of pseudo-oriental decoration was grafted onto western walls and western furniture. It was, of course, unthinkable that the Victorians should have stripped bare their rooms to resemble anything approaching true Japanese austerity.

In the process, however, some disconcerting changes took place. The 'Anglo-Japanese', as it was called, introduced a fashion for furniture as thin and skeletal as once it had been bulky and immobile. Bamboo was the medium employed – or imitation bamboo. (E. W. Godwin designed in 1868 a coffee table in ebonised wood in imitation of bamboo.) William Morris disapproved, declaring that furniture 'should be made of timber rather than walking sticks'. How far, one wonders, was this furniture influenced by the scientifically designed Thonet bentwood chairs which went into quantity production about 1859?

The 'Japanese' was far from being an academic style: a contemporary wrote, 'if one understands Japanese art one will prove to have experienced taste; the ideas will come, originality will put in an appearance and one will know how to furnish a house'. It is hardly surprising therefore that it should have appealed to the more adventurous spirits such as Godwin and Christopher Dresser. The former was studying Japanese examples as early as 1860 and Dresser paid a visit to Japan in 1876, under the influence of which he became an outspoken advocate of abstract form at the expense of ornament, even proposing the elimination of all drapery, including curtains, from the fashionable drawing room.

The word 'elimination' provides a key to the transition from the High Victorian to the *Fin-De-Siècle*: elimination of excess weight in furniture, elimination of some of the movable pieces themselves in favour of fixed fittings and finally elimination of some of the carefully-maintained barriers between the separate compartments in a house, making possible the ductile space we associate with the twentieth century.

The return to built-in furniture after three centuries had far-reaching effects: forcing an integration of the architecture and the furnishings which was of equal service to both. Library fittings, as static features, were naturally among the first to be absorbed: fitted sideboards and fixed settees or 'cozy corners' as they were called following suit. The result could be exciting spatially, creating enclosures within the larger room; the fashionable inglenook sometimes assuming the dimensions of a small room in itself.

Oddly enough, the vogue for fitted alcoves produced a short-lived Moorish revival during the 1880s, and this was especially evident in otherwise orthodox hotel designs, since the alcove was considered an indispensable attribute of that style. Lord Leighton fostered

the taste by inserting an Arabian Hall into his house at Holland Park, London.

With twentieth-century hindsight, the change which seems most significant to us is the opening up of the domestic plan. Richard Norman Shaw, the English architect and H. H. Richardson in America had each experimented by the year 1870 with the idea of a central-galleried living space from which stairs and the smaller rooms opened at two levels. The development of this idea depended on the acceptance of the principle of central heating, so that in the States, where thermal control was essential in any case, greater progress was made and readier acceptance was found.

The open treatment was ironically reintroduced to Europe as an American idea, a contemporary writing: 'in the States the *entresol* and staircase are often elegantly appointed'. In 1876 the English designer Bruce Talbert published schemes which showed the staircase opening from the dining-room with only a wide draped archway separating the two and it is clear that, from this time onwards, once the means were available to achieve an open plan without discomfort, designers and their clients were swift to exploit them.

Parallel with these changes in planning came the revolutionary ideas of the English Arts and Crafts designers. Of Morris, Pevsner wrote: 'we owe it to him that an ordinary man's dwelling house has once more become a worthy object of the architect's thought and a chair, a wallpaper or a vase a worthy object of the artist's imagination.' Morris put it more succinctly: 'Have nothing in your houses which you do not know to be useful or believe to be beautiful' – a sentiment which was to secure him a place of honour in the history of the Modern Movement and which links the tastes of the nineteenth century to those of the twentieth.

Milligan House, Saratoga Springs, New York

The parlour, beautifully reconstructed in the Brooklyn Museum. This room is typical of a prosperous middle-class interior of the mid 1850s: the plain walls and the slatted shutters are characteristically American details

49 Princes Gate, London

The Peacock Room. Painted by James McNeill Whistler in 1876–7 for the wealthy ship-owner and art collector F. R. Leyland, the work brought about a complete rift between artist and client. The whole room was eventually bought in 1904 by the Freer Gallery of Art in Washington

Penrhyn Castle,
Caernarvonshire,
Wales

opposite. *This drawing room
is an unusual essay in the
neo-Norman style; designed
by Thomas Hopper and
completed in the 1830s, this
room belongs in date to the
previous chapter, but it
displays so many characteristics of 'High Victorian' that it
has been included here*

Aranjuez Palace, near Madrid

*The smoking-room or Gabinete Arabe. Another piece of nineteenth-century romanticism, it makes an interesting
comparison with Lord Leighton's Arab Hall, shown in the next chapter*

Reform Club, London

Detail of the library. This brilliant building, completed by Barry in 1840, set the fashion in Italianate buildings for the next thirty years. The atmosphere of the interior – grand, scholarly and rich – admirably suited a club for gentlemen wielding considerable political influence

The Ristorante del Cambio, Turin, Italy. A charming interior, completed about 1850 to designs by Panizza

The grand saloon of the Mississippi steamer Grand Republic, *of about 1855, one of the most incredible interiors ever created. The seemingly endless vista of Victorian parlour suites down the centre of the floor creates an atmosphere of dreamlike fantasy*

Goldsmiths Hall, London

The Livery Hall – the grandest hall of the richest company, completed in 1835 to designs of Philip Hardwick in the most full-blooded nineteenth-century manner. The bust of George IV is by Chantrey

above. The Moorish sitting-room, from the house of
John D. Rockefeller, 4 West 54th Street, New York.
Very much belonging to the second half of the century,
this is the most exciting amalgam of rich colour and
unexpected shapes, and must have been the 'dernier
cri' at the time

opposite. Although not begun until 1885, the Walter
Gresham house at Galveston, Texas, USA has very
much the same feeling as the previous example.
The architect was Nicholas J. Clayton

Schloss Herrenchiemsee, Bavaria

The dining room in a castle built for King Ludwig II of Bavaria to designs of Georg Dollman. The interior decoration of the castle was carried out by Julius Hofmann, and this room, completed about 1884, was based on French precedent
The ceiling makes a fascinating comparison with that of the Salon Ovale in the Hôtel de Soubise, Paris

Schloss Linderhof, Bavaria

opposite. *The mirror room, in another castle built for Ludwig II, and completed in 1879. Endless vistas are created for the inhabitants of this room by cleverly juxtaposed mirrors. The lapis lazuli framed fireplaces, the crystal and ivory chandeliers, the gilt sofas covered in silk interwoven with silver thread and an ostrich-down rug, combine to make this room a fantastic creation*

Queen Victoria's Railway Carriage, London

Queen Victoria's private railway carriage, built by the London and North-Western Railway in 1869. above. *The view from the luxurious day saloon into the sergeant-footman's compartment* above right. *The end of the day saloon. The internal fittings were of a slightly conservative character for the period, but all the workmanship was of the very best and the detailing is remarkable* right. *An embroidered window-strap in the Royal Saloon. This elaborated device pulls up over an ivory pivot set in a carved ivory capping*

Château de Grosbois, near Fontainebleau, France

opposite. *In deference to the most illustrious owner of the house, Maréchal Berthier, a number of specifically 'Empire' elements were introduced into the decorative scheme for this library*

Château de Ferrières, Seine et Marne, France

The castle was completed by the early 1860s for Baron James de Rothschild, and this salon combines beautifully many of the rich elements of the prosperous home of the period

Cardiff Castle, Glamorganshire, Wales

This extraordinary building was designed by William Burges and constructed during the years 1865–81 for Lord Bute. The interior contains a fascinating riot of carving, colour, pattern and strange shapes, and the Tower room shown here is one of the most remarkable
opposite. Detail of painted carved work in the Tower room

The chandelier, the gallery and the lantern in the Tower room at Cardiff Castle. Burges' skill extended to the design of furniture and fittings and all of his few buildings are enhanced by them

Youssoupoff Palace, Leningrad

The private theatre, constructed within the eighteenth–century building during the alterations, and carried out under the direction of Stepanoff during the latter part of the nineteenth century. The neo–Louis XV style was still considered de rigueur for the interiors of very grand houses during the whole of the second half of the century

FIN-DE-SIÈCLE 1880-1920

Ashley Barker

By the last quarter of the nineteenth century the great room as a distinct art form had entered into a period of marked decline. At least this is true within the domestic sphere which is for the moment our principal area of examination, although if we were considering more closely the field of public buildings the statement would be rather open to question. The closing years of the old century and the first decade of the present one represented a great period for the construction of public and municipal buildings all over Europe and these were furnished with ambitious, if not universally successful, halls and apartments. Moreover, the period was not one which showed any lack of invention or of quality over the wider range of architectural production. The picture was certainly confused at times and there may have been some lack of direction and even of confidence amongst the more thoughtful practitioners of architecture and decoration, but there was enormous creativeness and vigour displayed in tackling the host of problems new to architecture in this increasingly turbulent epoch.

Why then should we detect such a decline in the creation of great rooms in the major houses of the time? The failure which we diagnose seems due not so much to any lack of ability on the part of the artists and designers as to a reluctance to attempt the problem at all, even amongst those building the most ambitious new houses; a reluctance on the part of the owner and designer alike. That this was a consciously recognised state of affairs we may learn from contemporary sources. In the opening year of our notional *Fin-de-Siècle* period J. J. Stevenson, a leading London architect who specialised in the field of house design, published a book which gives us numerous insights into the situation as he saw it. He wrote:

Of the artistic effects of architecture many, such especially as grandeur or sublimity, would be out of place in ordinary houses. They are attainable in palaces; some of which, notably those of Florence, are as impressive in their architecture as great religious buildings.

Nowadays palaces generally are only larger houses to accommodate a large establishment. State and grandeur have become irksome to us, and are even despised, no doubt because so frequently they are the sign of power which has departed; and the sense of power consequently

opposite. The Arab Hall, Leighton House, London, introduced in 1880 into the house that Lord Leighton had built for himself in 1865. It was predictable that one of the most fashionable painters of the day should have constructed his new room with many genuine old tiles and other elements brought from the near East, in accordance with the passion for antiques and imitation of the past

seems more exquisite to us when unemcumbered by its trappings. Comfort and convenience are all that are insisted on.

This change is not advantageous to the development of the highest type of domestic architecture.

There had been no such suggestion in, for example, Robert Kerr's remarkably comprehensive book on house design published only fifteen years earlier. In that work the sections devoted to the design of state rooms make it abundantly clear that 'state and grandeur' were by no means irksome in Kerr's view. But if grandeur was on the way out in 1880 there is no doubt about the insistence on comfort.

It has been reserved for our age to find out that beauty in our dwellings is not worth striving for, that material wants are all that need be attended to.

Now the great room does not come about from an attempt to fulfil 'material wants' or to attain 'comfort and convenience'. In common with other forms of art it has much more of the character of a celebration. In a house this celebration reflects its owner's standing, aspirations and delight in life. If then in 1880 the tradition of Great Rooms was slowly dying what changes in circumstances could have been causing the failure to celebrate through monumental house interiors?

It may be helpful in pursuing this line of thought to bear in mind the definition of monument as 'an indication, evidence or token'. A major house in the preceding years had given material form to the traditions and standing of a particular family in a particular place. The idea of family continuity required an expression of permanence whilst its cultural ideals and traditions of taste and learning required demonstration through the skilful use of certain specific and accepted architectural forms. The family wealth and power were shown in architectural display, with precious materials elaborately wrought within the accepted disciplines. With all this the creators of such splendours stamped their character on a particular place, making the place unique and the centre of their lives, but by 1880 we may detect certain changes relevant to our subject.

Let us consider the matter of place first. Where previously the celebration of place and the unique association of a family with a particular district had been of prime importance, the coming of swift and above all comfortable transport was beginning to break down the importance attached to locality. If there was to be a celebration in 1880 it was more likely to be a celebration of rapid travel rather than of the virtues of a particular place. It is certainly no accident that two of the interiors illustrated here are in fact travelling interiors – from a train and a ship. The full appreciation of a great room requires time to be spent in tranquillity whilst its glories and embellishments are explored. It makes no impact on the restless man caught up in the desire to travel and just off to catch his train. Ruskin had appreciated this point some years earlier when he wrote:

Another of the strange and evil tendencies of the present day is to the decoration of the rail-road station. Now, if there be any place in the world in which people are deprived of that portion of temper and discretion which are necessary to the contemplation of beauty, it is there. It is the very temple of discomfort. . . . The whole system of rail-road travelling is addressed to people who, being in a hurry, are therefore for the time being, miserable. . . . Rail-road architecture has, or would have, a dignity of its own if it were only left to its work.

The essential monuments to travel then were such things as the gateway through which one passed into the magic world of swift travel, the train shed and the viaduct, although some were fortunate enough to take their private room travelling with them.

Even within this field and over a short period a comparison of the interior of King Edward VII's coach on the LNWR with that of Queen Victoria's coach from the same railway, shows an increased acceptance of the essential travelling character as distinct from the static monumental character of the earlier example. The Victorian coach is a tiny though grand drawing room on wheels. The Queen actively disliked rapid travel. The Edwardian interior on the other hand was intentionally 'like the cabin of a ship' – the traditional travelling interior.

Just as there is less insistence on the celebration of place so there is also less insistence on the celebration of permanence.

As Ruskin had seen the cause to attack railways and the worship of speed in *The Lamp of Beauty* he had also seen it necessary to attack impermanence in *The Lamp of Memory* –

. . . it is in becoming memorial or monumental that a true perfection is attained by civil and domestic buildings. . . . I cannot but think it an evil sign of a people when their houses are built to last for one generation only. There is a sanctity in a good man's house which cannot be renewed in every tenement that rises on its ruins. . . .

The rapid increase in population with the inevitable change in balance between old and new houses at all levels of society may have itself done something to lessen the sense of

Design for the decoration of the coffee room at the Union Club, London, by J. G. Crace, 1889. A successful example of the type of linear stencilled decoration popularised as far back as the 1860s

continuity between family and house and if we are to associate the great room with the concept of monument, as I suggest we must, then the onset of the failure to desire and celebrate permanence is another of the seeds of decay.

Change and variety rather than permanence were the popular virtues amongst the house builders and their architects in 1880 and if variety was in demand then the archaeologists, the explorers and the travellers (and again we must remark the importance of travel) had a stock of new delights to offer – a knowledge of styles and buildings such as no age ever had before. Through their meticulous measured drawings and the ever more popular cult of the sketch book old buildings were recorded so accurately that they might be reproduced in every detail. If a man wished to demonstrate his taste and wide knowledge in architectural terms, it was overwhelmingly tempting to venture further and further into the exotic styles and nowhere more so than in the field of interior design. Where grandeur had become irksome and refinement within the previously accepted styles boring, then owner and artist alike were off to pursue the exotic, the fantastic and the hybrid. If they gained in variety they inevitably lost the deep inner understanding which is the hallmark of the slow growth of tradition. Where tradition was seen as moribund and boring many no doubt would have considered the price well while. One result of this circumstance was that the owner and his artist concerned themselves as they had never done before as to what style would be most appropriate, not only for a particular building, but for a particular room. As the number of acceptable styles increased, the choice of a style with appropriate associations as a vehicle for a particular architectural expression became more and more subtle. This enormous vocabulary so often derided in the intervening years was in one sense a great strength in the architecture of the period. It gave the designers that flexibility needed to cover the unprecedented problem in new building types which confronted them in this most trying period. The exploitation of a variety of styles in complex adaptations and intermixtures made possible a delicacy of evocation and expression which the period since the First World War has all too seldom provided.

Nevertheless it was a state of affairs which led to introspection –

. . . Is it possible for us to confine ourselves to one style? Certainly no imperial enactment would make us do so, much less any councils or persuasions in books.

There are probably too many opposing modes of thought at present for one style to be a suitable expression of them all. Neither the social conditions nor the philosophy are yet born which can bring unity into thought and into art. Nor can we delay building our houses and cities till this happens.

All the styles of the world are open for us to choose from.

The existence of such a variety of styles was not a reason nor a central factor in the failure to create great rooms, but it had become more important in house building to seek out a new taste or a new flavour rather than to create a monument. The flavours could be rare and exotic, they were certainly very varied and the skill of the cooks was much to be admired – they simply had less and less desire to attempt the great. The extraordinarily varied range of *Fin-de-Siècle* house interiors which resulted can be a source of much pleasure and can certainly give scope for connoisseurship of the more esoteric kind. Nevertheless the impermanence, the search after novelty, the restlessness and the self-consciousness in seeking the appropriate style are all aspects of decay so far as our present study is concerned and they are the *Fin-de-Siècle* characteristics.

In fields other than house building the concepts of monumentality and grandeur still had some meaning. It was, as we have already noted, a great age of public buildings – of town halls, hotels, theatres and civic buildings of all kinds in Europe and America alike. Public bodies from governments to small town corporations were engaging eagerly in erecting all sorts of buildings, 'almost all of them with some attempt at architectural magnificence'. In these categories and perhaps most of all in America the great room had a continued lease of life and it is this reflection which brings us back to the point at which we started in the domestic context and which is after all the real key to the matter – 'State and grandeur have become irksome to us, and are even despised.'

The expression of personal status, however, is hardly to be dispensed with as easily as that. If state and grandeur had become irksome then there were other ways of demonstrating personal wealth and power. Such possessions as the private railway carriage, the steam yacht and even the motor car not only conferred status, but also celebrated at the altar of speed and travel; whilst still within the house the same restlessness found expression in a multiplicity of rooms which could be varied in style, each dedicated to a separate activity. As we turn the pages of the architectural periodicals – which by this period give us a minute picture of architectural affairs – we find not great state rooms in the new houses of the wealthy but billiards rooms and smoking rooms, often commodious rather than beautiful. A substantial house of the 1880s, in addition to its two or more drawing

The first-class smoking room of the steamer Oceanic. This interior was designed by R. Norman Shaw, one of the most successful English architects of his day, in 1900, and despite the fixed seats, it displays a very close affinity with the fashionable house interior

rooms, might well boast music room, billiards room, gentlemen's room, smoking room, gun room and more. Even the Edwardian royal coach after all had its smoking room. Certain critics were again doubtful as to the wisdom of these trends.

Empty rooms make a dreary house; nor does a great number of public rooms contribute to privacy, for there is no real retirement in apartments open to all the family and guests, and even on occasion to servants. It is better with the increase of the household to increase the size rather than the number of the public rooms.

The advice fell on deaf ears. Where state and grandeur are undesirable it is natural enough to seek subdivision into small compartments since to build a large room is to call for expressions of state, whereas small rooms may be 'attractive', 'tasteful' and 'pretty'. It might be interesting to put the question in parenthesis at this point whether the influence of the emancipated woman on house decorating and furnishing did not play some part in championing the pretty against the grand as our period proceeded.

Nevertheless if we are approaching the end of the road there is still much to be enjoyed. Luxury and ephemeral pleasures may have superseded monumentality but what a delightful showing they could make. 'The tendency', said a writer in *The. Studio* in 1897 with particular reference to the productions of the Tiffany Studio in New York, 'is to grace and worldliness rather than dignity and austerity . . .' and the words seem to contain the essence of the era.

It is already apparent from the foregoing that we can no longer follow one or two comparatively simple strands in the development of taste to form a picture of the *Fin-de-Siècle*

FIN-DE-SIÈCLE

interior. The developments in the last quarter of the century are terribly complex. To appreciate this extraordinary diversity in styles we must realise how much stemmed from the perpetual struggle to avoid boredom. The increase in the wealth of nations and even more in the number of people with a substantial share in this affluence meant a great increase in the number of substantial (if not great) interiors to be created. Easy travel once again and, particularly by the end of the century the illustrated journals, meant that a man might be familiar with such a range of rooms and types of rooms throughout a number of countries that the invention of something new and interesting was becoming more and more difficult. Palates were jaded and the opportunity to explore and re-explore the historic and exotic styles in search of something fresh became irresistibly tempting. The parallel with cooking is particularly apt since the rapidity of production of substantial rooms was almost akin to the production of menus always posing the problem of how to produce something different to tempt the flagging appetite.

It may be that the machine products and the possibility of endless inferior copies of each piece of art work also played their part in the general process of aesthetic devaluation, but it was not only the multiplication of the copy or the inferior article that led to boredom and satiation.

A man with the wealth which Baron Ferdinand de Rothschild had at his command when he commissioned the building of his new mansion at Waddesdon (1874–89), could assemble a collection of art works of such magnificence that the thought of further addition to the rooms and their furnishings becomes pointless. Everything at Waddesdon was of superlative quality – house, rooms and contents. They bring us just to the point of balance where wealth becomes oppressive, the very point at which state and grandeur become irksome. The rooms are filled with a perfection of furniture, *boiseries*, tapestries and *objets d'art* and with such technical perfection achieved the need for further effort disappears. We can hardly be sure how much they are *Fin-de-Siècle* rooms and how much a collection. It is a characteristic of rooms like these of the last quarter of the century that not only do they draw on various historical styles but they may also incorporate, not only in furnishings but in the fabric, actual materials and craft-work taken from original examples of the styles adopted. Designed by Gabriel-Hippolyte Destailleur, this Chiltern mansion adopts architectural motifs from Chambord and Blois assembled with great skill by its experienced academic architect, but more than that the interiors are lined with Parisian eighteenth-century *boiseries*, from the Hôtel de Lauzun (the Grey Drawing Room), from the Hôtel de Richelieu (the Breakfast Room), from the Villa Beaujon (the Tower Room), and so on, whilst the marble-lined dining-room incorporates splendid carved mirrors from the Hôtel de Villars. Finally in an extreme case in the Green Boudoir of this house we find ourselves in a room which is a complete mid-eighteenth century room of great beauty but owing nothing to the period around 1880 except for the fact of its removal and reincorporation. Like the *boiseries* of the Breakfast Room it came from the Hôtel de Richelieu in Paris. Modern transport was making such international interchange of building parts possible along with all its other benefits to mankind! Apart from the Green Boudoir at Waddesdon, however, we are in rooms which for all their

borrowing are rooms essentially of the last quarter of the nineteenth century with its special characteristics. State and grandeur certainly still exist here, but we sense that they will never reach this peak again and we sense much of the reasons. Only another Rothschild such as Baron Alfred Charles at nearby Halton House with his splendid white and gold hall could challenge this sort of display. A less wealthy man out to make an impression and up against this sort of thing could only seek his effects by novelty and so along with the increasing variety of traditional and resurrected European styles came the eastern and oriental modes suitable for those with consciously aesthetic leanings.

Sir Frederick Leighton, the celebrated painter (for one), adopted the Moorish style when he added to his house in Kensington in 1880. His great room was only some 25 feet square and accomplished at a fraction of the effort and outlay which went into Waddesdon, but by its exotic form it must have made as great an impact in its way. Of the eastern styles Moorish never looked like rivalling the wide influence of Japanese art but nevertheless it had its adherents and in such a case as this it was eminently suited to impress the sitters of a great painter. Leighton's architect for the work was Professor George Aitchison who built the house to which it formed an addition some fifteen years earlier and is said to have made special studies for this room in 'Moorish Spain'. As at Waddesdon, authenticity is added by the importation of actual elements of the adopted style, this time in the form of tiles and wooden screens. Leighton's room is a triumph of art for art's sake, adding little to the accommodation of the house but greatly increasing its architectural effect – the essential great room in fact. Opening out of the staircase compartment through a low ante-room without doors and arranged so that all visitors to the house must catch a glimpse of the romantic vista into it on arrival, the Arab Hall is a tall domed chamber, the centre of which is occupied by a rectangular pool edged in black marble with a single fountain jet. The entry, flanked with paired corinthian columns of Brocatello marble with luxuriant gilded capitals, occupies one side of the square plan whilst the three remaining sides are given shallow transepts set beneath pointed arches carried on slender inset corinthian columns. Pendentives of Arabic form across the angles between the transepts reduce the compartment to an octagon on which sits a circular dome. Thus if the intention and decoration are exotic the form is severely architectural. The floor of black and white marble has the character of an ambulatory around the pool emphasising the symmetry of the centralised plan, but the glory of the room lies in the collection of sixteenth- and seventeenth-century Syrian tiles, which line the principal wall surfaces. Together with the carved wooden screens of Damascus lattice work which cover the windows and guard a gallery opening from the first floor, these tiles and a quantity of stained glass were brought back from the Middle East at Leighton's request. The decoration is given additional unity by a great frieze running into the transepts and beneath the pendentives with birds and animals on a gold mosaic ground designed by Walter Crane. The alabaster capitals of the inset corinthian columns were carved by Sir Edgar Boehm and the birds in the capitals of the columns at the entrance were modelled by Randolph Caldecott. The effect is at once rich, artistic and self-consciously exotic. Although not large in size (and even then with the floor largely taken up with a pool) this room with all its art work, both imported and purpose made, turns Leighton's modest house into an eastern palace for at least as long as the uncertain Kensington sun filters through the Damascus beadwork onto the tiles and the pool; but as surely as with Waddesdon we may feel that this room, fascinating as it is, is just another by-way of taste offering no real road forward into the future.

Through the last two decades of the old century English domestic architecture was to play a leading and influential part in European development and to gain some idea of the aspects of English work which were to have this effect we shall do better to look at such a room as Norman Shaw's gallery at Cragside. The way forward in fact lay with Shaw, with Philip Webb who had preceded Shaw as chief assistant in G. E. Street's office and

The Directors' Room, New York Life Insurance Company, New York City. McKim, Mead and White, 1897. All this architectural firm's mastery is shown here in a room which, although in a commercial building, has a certain domestic character

with Eden Nesfield with whom Shaw had entered into partnership from about 1862 to 1868. Shaw was to be the leading house architect in England for at least two-thirds of our period. From the Gothic climate of Street's office, never well adapted to domestic purposes, Shaw moved steadily over the course of thirty years or so through great houses in Tudor and Jacobean forms (which have been christened Shavian Manorial) through his Anglo-Dutch and so called 'Queen Anne' innovations towards the Neo-classicism which he was to reach about his sixtieth year. For the earlier of his country houses Shaw designed great halls of medieval form with open timber roofs such as those at Merrist Wood (1877), Pierrepoint (1876) and Dawpool (1882). The Cragside Gallery dates from 1880–2 and was an addition to the house built by Shaw ten years earlier for the first Lord Armstrong, the Newcastle Steel Master – one of his earliest works. The room which he provided for the accommodation of his Lordship's pictures is one in which he moves on to the style of the Elizabethan Renaissance. It is dominated by its vast fireplace, the riotous invention in the carved alabaster frieze to the fire opening and in the great overmantel stretching up into the eliptical vault of the ceiling, being inspired by Elizabethan Mannerist examples. This enrichment covers the deep coves flanking the lay-light by which the room is illuminated with strapwork and arabesques, but the effect of the gallery, rich as the surface decoration may be, is completely opposed to the stiff formality of the rooms at Waddesdon and to the incommodious exoticism of Leighton's Arab Hall. In an age when state and grandeur had become irksome but comfort still required a monumental setting, we may feel happy that Shaw had provided his client with everything he could wish for in this comfortable, robust, grand and yet informal room. Such a critic as Heathcote Statham writing in 1897 could regret the lack of '. . . dignity and nobility in the

Design for the hall of a country house, by Baillie Scott & Seton Morris, 1895. A good complete interior in the manner generally associated with Voysey, of the peasant craft tradition which stems originally from William Morris

modern picturesque as represented even in so good an example as Cragside'. Nevertheless even he had to admit '. . . if it is desired that the prominent characteristic of a dwelling however large should be that of homeliness it is here doubtless attained'.

We can well understand Shaw's prodigious success as he pursues his course on from rooms like these through the 'Queen Anne' manner (which again could provide just the desired qualities) towards the Edwardian Classical of his later years. Just as his fluent invention never fails, he provides his clients with houses nicely judged to their needs, status and way of life in the most fashionable style of the time – which was of course whichever style he was working in! A great part of his genius was the ability to develop the appropriate styles and to mould them to suit the various facets of the spirit of the age. Shaw's influence on English house building was greater than that of any other architect of his time. J. J. Stevenson, whose opinions I have already quoted, Sir Ernest George, A. H. Mackmurdo, C. F. A. Vosey, C. R. Ashbee and many other distinguished architects took their inspiration from one aspect or another of Shaw's work, so building a powerful school of English designers which was in turn to influence the European continent.

Well before the middle of the century, English and European critics had been disturbed by what they saw as the lack of a central style or characteristic nineteenth-century tradition. At the opening meeting of the Architectural Association in London in 1847 Professor Donaldson had said, 'the great question is are we to have an architecture of our period, a distinct, individual, palpable style of the nineteenth century'. The cry became more and more insistent as the century wore on, to reach a crescendo in the final quarter, but even so all those concerned were not looking in the same direction. Ruskin had complained in the *Seven Lamps of Architecture* that no day passed without English architects being called on to invent a new style and he reacted firmly to the suggestion. He wrote:

There seems to me to be a wonderful misunderstanding among the majority of architects at the present day as to the very nature and meaning of Originality, and of all wherein it consists. Originality in expression does not depend on invention of new words: nor Originality in poetry on invention of new measures; nor, in painting, on invention of new colours, or new modes of using them. The chords of music, the harmonies of colour, the general principles of the arrangement of sculptured masses, have been determined long ago, and in all probability, cannot be added to any more than they can be altered. Granting that they may be, such additions or alterations are much more the work of time and of multitudes than of individual inventors.

For all Ruskin's words and in spite of the fact that in all the stylistic languages adopted, the nineteenth century now appears to us to have demonstrated a consistency of attitude which transmuted them into something unique and essentially its own, nevertheless the striving to create a new non-derivative style was insistent. Some critics and practitioners felt that there had been a point in history where the path had been missed. Others sought a new style by mixing inherited ones.

Arts and Crafts Movement

At all events during the 1880s in England a new growth began to appear in the form of the Arts and Crafts Movement, which again was to have a wide influence in Europe. Inspired by the work of William Morris, this was in essence an attempt to return not so much to an earlier style in hope of retrieving the threads as to get back to an earlier medieval pre-machine attitude towards craft work, more particularly as related to the design of houses and their interiors and furnishings. Its apostles were keen to re-establish the old ideals of hand craftsmanship in a union of all of the branches of arts, crafts and building, and to seek a way out of the trap, as they saw it, of derivative styles. It was not of course a completely non-derivative style itself. If it adopted the philosophy of going back and starting again, it also adopted the practice of mixing from a variety of English medieval and post-medieval sources. Now the emergence of such an attitude to design should lead us to take heart in our search for great rooms, because here are ideals to celebrate, legitimate monumental ideals such as joy in permanence, in craftsmanship and in developing tradition, delight in fine materials and delight in fine works of the past. Here too was an interest in the associated arts of embellishment, in pattern making for papers and fabrics, in painted decoration, glass and so on, all to be united under architectural guidance. The fact that the skill in pattern design and the two-dimensional decoration of surfaces was one of the greatest achievements of the movement did not prevent a kind of austerity which percolated the whole of its productions. This was natural as part of the reaction against the growing Victorian tendency to make surfaces and outlines richer and richer and more and more complicated whatever the style. The key attributes of the new celebration were honesty, sincerity and a rediscovery which at times looks like simplicity. This apparent austerity is not the result of a puritanical outlook which

would tend to oppose the act of celebration, but rather the simplifying effect of a return to more direct sources of inspiration and the cutting away of accumulated habits of design. It may be for this reason that the Arts and Crafts Movement is usually treated as one of the foundation stones of 'Modern Architecture'. That relationship is not, however, one of direct descent. It lay through the influence of the English work on German designers such as Peter Behrens who were impressed by what they saw as its matter-of-fact reasonableness. Between 1896 and 1903 Hermann Muthesius was attached to the German Embassy in London with a brief to carry out research on English housing and thus became a sort of channel of influence between London and Germany where the 'modern movement' was to emerge. England was to play hardly any part in this emergence and it seems open to doubt whether the admittedly far-reaching effect of the arts and crafts tradition entitles us to place this movement with all its anti-machine connotations as a true precursor of 'modern' design. Indeed Van de Velde, the Dutch protagonist of functional aesthetics, regarded it as a pastime of highly sensitive artists for sensitive connoisseurs – inbred and a dead end. Nevertheless its wide-reaching influence is undeniable and English designers were receiving important continental commissions, such as the work of Baillie Scott for the Grand Duke of Hesse in Darmstadt in 1898. Whatever its subsequent influences the tradition itself remained wholly of the old order and of the nineteenth century. The approach of such architects as Philip Webb, unconventional as it then seemed, was based firmly on a direct understanding of traditional methods – that was its essential strength. It was in no way looking forward to the age of synthetic materials and industrialised buildings. In looking at such uncompromising statements made with such confidence as those in Webb's rooms at 'Clouds' we are convinced that we are in the presence of a new tradition of domestic monument building which in its slow steady growth must provide a way forward. Lutyens later recorded that in about 1891, when he first began to be influenced by the work of Philip Webb, then in his sixtieth year, its freshness and originality caused him in ignorance to attribute the work to a young man.

Art Nouveau

During the 1890s the phenomenon now generally known as *Art Nouveau* swept Europe as the style of advanced fashion. It arose out of the same basic desire as the Arts and Crafts Movement which must have made substantial contribution to its birth but was more extreme and frenetic in its attempt to create a new anti-historical style. The desire for novelty for·its own sake and the desire to satisfy the philosophical yearning to sever all reliance on the past were obviously pulling strongly together. If the Arts and Crafts Movement has its feet firmly on medieval precedent, *Art Nouveau* was less securely based. It spread all over Europe with such startling rapidity that no one seemed quite certain where it could have come from – least of all the English who had contributed so largely to its inception. Again, the ease of travel and the dissemination of ideas through the illustrated journals such as *The Studio*, *Pan*, *Jugend*, *L'Art Decoratif*, *Ver Sacrum*, and others, were vital factors. The movement had perhaps two prime movers, Louis Sullivan in Chicago and Victor Horta in Brussels, and sparked off by the work of these men *Art Nouveau* became a craze which, even if one dates it from such a building as Sullivan's Auditorium Building built in Chicago in 1888, burned itself out in under twenty years.

For all its boast of originality and professed anti-historical orientation, *Art Nouveau* was still dependent on precedent but by now the contributory threads were so complex as to make detailed analysis extremely difficult; perhaps more so than with any other

Design for the drawing room chimney-piece at 8 Addison Road, London, by Halsey Ricardo in 1905-8. This fascinating house, built for Debenham the store-owner, displays throughout the questing and inventive mind of its architect

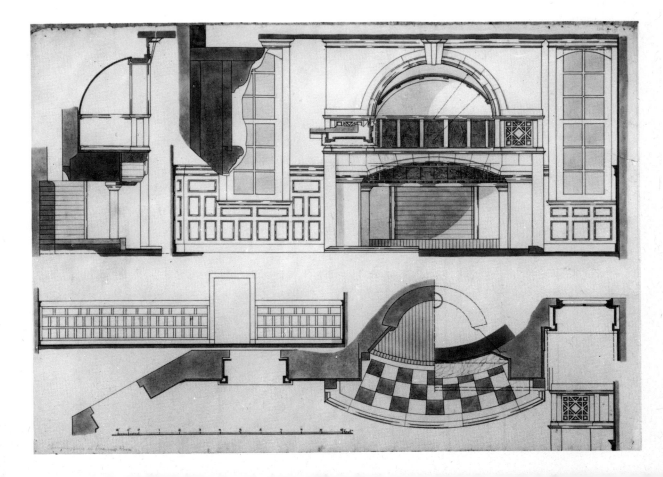

FIN-DE-SIÈCLE

comparable movement in the history of architecture and decoration. Recent writers have drawn attention to such diverse tributaries as the stylistic influences of Rococo, Gothic, the effect of Japanese and Celtic decorative forms and even such factors as the art of William Blake. These and other strands – some of the more central ones already united by the Arts and Crafts Movement – were woven into a style which was curiously coherent considering its make-up and which did at first examination appear more or less non-derivative because the sources were so many and so mixed.

The central and unique characteristic of the style lay in the use of a sinuous flowing line which may be seen as akin to waves or flames or to the tendrils of growing plants. In Belgium they knew it as 'coup de fouet' or 'paling' (whiplash or eel style) for this reason.

If I was right in suggesting earlier that published illustrations and travel were instrumental in causing the search for novelty and variety to reach such an intense pitch, it seems all the more certain that the same factors tended to make the solution remarkably uniform not only over Europe but in America too. Along with these influences went the increasing popularity of the great international exhibitions of applied arts in ensuring the uniform spread of the new ideas. The rooms which were illustrated in the periodicals were very largely show-rooms from these exhibitions. Because of the publicity they received and the influence which they had, they remain the first examples to spring to mind when we think of the *Art Nouveau* room. Such rooms as those designed by Van de Velde for M.S. Bing's shop in Paris and shown at Dresden in 1897, Riemerschmid's Music Room shown at the exhibition of German Art held in the same town in 1899 and Pankok's smoking-rooms exhibited in Paris at the exhibition of 1900, are amongst the most obvious examples of rooms in the style. Seen by thousands who would never have had access to them in a private house and reproduced in photographs in periodicals all over Europe and America, their influence was enormous. A design could even appear in more than one exhibition – as for example the Pankok smoking-room which re-appeared in the Turin International Exhibition of 1902.

These impermanent rooms were characteristic of a style which, like a great exhibition itself, flowered and died in such a short time. They show an interesting unity of decoration, furnishing and fittings which belong to an exhibit as distinct from a room in a house. The contributions of the various arts and crafts are closely knitted together but the central intention of an exhibition is of course commercial rather than monumental. These *Art Nouveau* rooms were to be bought rather than built or decorated. They are essentially unmonumental. It is significant that the very name *Art Nouveau* was taken from the name of a shop opened in Paris in the Rue de Provence in 1895 by M.S. Bing, a Hamburg art dealer, whilst in Italy the style was known as *Stile Liberty* after the shop in Regent Street, London.

However, amongst the work executed by Victor Horta, the initiator of the central stream of the style in Brussels from 1892 onwards, we do find rooms which cause us to take heart such as, for example, at the house of Baron van Eetvelde at 4 Avenue Palmerston, executed in 1895. Here in the salon, for all the strangeness of the style, is a measure of monumentality. As a centrally planned compartment – domed and with a raised ambulatory round a central well, it makes an interesting comparison with Leighton's Arab Hall from which it is separated by as little as 15 years. The growing plant forms with sinuous metallic tendrils give the room the quality of a conservatory or a palm house so that the potted plants which were placed within it united with the architecture and decoration into one living whole. The whole thing might, one feels, become the man-eating plant of science fiction ready to seize the unwary occupant with its rising tendrils. The metallic 'tree' stanchions send out branches which weave into the dome and the surrounding ambulatory vault, forms at once Gothic, oriental and essentially arboreal. The balustrades are formed of twisting tendrils and the electric lamps depend as glass flowers from sinuous metal stems. Yet all of this is fused into a balanced, coherent and even formal unity. We cannot but be impressed and excited by it, it has all the essential *Fin-de-Siècle* flavour and the fact that we know that it will flower for such a short time makes it particularly poignant for us.

But interiors such as those in the Avenue Palmerston were few.

The very factors which led to the creation of *Art Nouveau* and the nature of the style with its emphasis on change in novelty, made it unlikely to become a vehicle for the creation of great rooms on any scale. Certainly it was a less suitable medium than the Arts and Crafts Movement which was so much more firmly based on traditional, monumental ways of thought, materials and method. This is not to deny but rather to emphasise *Fin-de-Siècle* glamour of this evanescent style.

In spite of its short life the names of designers and others associated with *Art Nouveau* are legion, names each evocative of some aspect of *Art Nouveau* such as the glass of Louis Tiffany and of Emile Gallé, the jewellery of Lalique, the designers and architects such as Horta, van de Velde, Plumet, and Guimard the creator of the stations for the Paris Métro. There were Obrist, Endell, Riemershmidt and Pankok in Munich, Mackmurdo and Mackintosh in Great Britain, Charpentier the sculptor and furniture designer, Jourdain, who designed the Samaritaine Store in Paris and, greatest of all, the Catalan architect Antoni Gaudí.

The relationships and influences between all those concerned are extremely confused owing to the rapidity with which the ideas flashed across Europe, but one is left with the sense that the number of artists is out of all proportion both to the body of the work achieved and to the length of life of the movement. Henry-Russell Hitchcock has pointed out the 'excessive amount of invention that even a modest *Art Nouveau* structure requires', and these aspects are perhaps linked. When we are considering an era which showed such obsession with novelty and originality we appreciate more than ever the importance of a living tradition to which each artist adds a little and from the accumulated wealth of which he can draw. No style which lasted less than twenty years can develop very far, but *Art Nouveau* could not perhaps by its nature develop at all. Only in the works of Gaudí in Barcelona and Mackintosh in Glasgow did the influence of the style extend beyond its own limited confines and even in their work, for all their apartness from the main stream, precedent plays its vital part. Here at all events are two artists who, in different ways, pursued the aims of monumental

FIN-DE-SIÈCLE

design whether in the sumptuous rooms of Gaudí's Güell Palace with their Moorish affinities, or his post-*Art Nouveau* of the Casa Batlló, or in Mackintosh's Cranston Tea Rooms, or in the library of the Glasgow School of Art. The popularity of the style receded with great rapidity, leaving Mackintosh in particular a tragic figure, his commissions fading away at the height of his success. In his last years he built scarcely anything and by the years after 1910 the great Spaniard was left alone as the only figure with *Art Nouveau* associations who had not entirely severed connection with the style.

But great figures as these men were, they have taken us outside the main stream of production to which we must return. By 1911 F. M. Simpson could write with evident relief on the last page of his *History of Architectural Development*:

The art of stately planning is now returning and a more chastened version of classic has supplanted Queen Anne and the sketch book vagaries. Once again attention is being paid to the precepts of Palladio and the other great Italians of the sixteenth century, and to the works of Inigo Jones and Wren. The tendency became marked in the last decade of the last century and since then has daily been growing in volume. At first there were fears that this might prove but another phase that would 'fret its hour upon the stage' and then collapse, as other movements had collapsed. For a short time that seemed possible. A cry arose from a few that tradition was nought; that salvation lay in ignoring it. The advent of 'Art Nouveau' was a blessing in disguise; in as much as it showed how false the cry was. Its immediate result was to stiffen and consolidate the movement in the exactly opposite direction and to unite men who before had been at variance.

This progress 'back to Palladio' we have noted in the work of Norman Shaw and others, but its equivalent was to be found far earlier in America – as far back as the 1880s in the work of McKim, Mead and White who ought to be amongst the real heroes of this essay. From their buildings and perhaps theirs alone at this time we could fill volumes of examples of great rooms and find them in no way deficient in greatness.

Due, it seems, largely to the influence of their associate Joseph Merrill Wells, this firm led the reaction against the Romantic picturesque forms exemplified in the massive Romanesque style of H. H. Richardson which had until then been in the ascendancy and turned their faces towards the Italian High Renaissance. Through such buildings as the Villard houses in Madison Avenue of 1882 and subsequently the Boston public library and many other Classical designs, McKim, Mead and White led this American reaction a decade in advance of Norman Shaw and his British contemporaries. The establishment of a strong *beaux arts* tradition in New York – whilst Norman Shaw, Sir Ernest George, T. E. Colcutt and others worked their way more slowly towards the state of affairs which F. M. Simpson was to find so agreeable – provided an ideal medium for the production of great rooms in a country where state and grandeur had not yet become irksome.

To this great firm, for we encounter here clearly the work of a group rather than that of a person, the opportunity came to build on the scale of ancient Rome. In 1926 C. H. Reilly predicted that future generations would look at their work '. . . as we do now at the work of the great Italian Giants'. We may now agree that his prediction is coming

true. At the turn of the century then America was the country where the great room was still a natural and flourishing expression. Critics have praised the taste, the scholarship and the restraint of these Americans even in their most ambitious projects where invention could so easily have outrun caution. Back in Europe there was certainly no shortage of caution. As the old century expired, Heathcote Statham wrote:

Of late the *nouveaux riches* have grown so knowing that they will sometimes consciously adopt the quiet and unassuming style of domestic architecture, which they have discovered represents the taste of an older class of society, just as they will desire to rent a small house in Mayfair rather than a big one in Portland Place.

The *folie de petitesse* in house design had become all-absorbing! And so we must look to hotels, clubs, ships and board rooms for our examples.

In London at the turn of the century the productions of the emerging Neo-classical school were certainly less pure and generally less grand than those of McKim, Mead and White, but at the same time they were interestingly varied in their approach and offer a rich field for analysis. Interiors such as those produced by T. E. Colcutt for *Lloyds Register of Shipping*, for instance, bringing together the influences of the Arts and Crafts and *Art Nouveau* with the emerging Edwardian Classical, seemed to possess the quintessential *Fin-de-Siècle* flavour. If a single symbol were to be sought to epitomise the best of these years, F. Lynn Jenkins's frieze to the stair and his decoration in bronze and ivory which surmounts the newel would be amongst the most suitable candidates. If the monuments of Rome had inspired J. M. Wells in New York, London designers such as Sir Ernest George and Peto had a catholic taste which would allow them to be influenced by sources as diverse as the Florentine Quattrocento and various forms of Spanish Renaissance as well as more northern European sources. Arthur J. Davis on the other hand was predominantly, although not exclusively, French in his outlook. Like McKim he was French educated and trained at the *École des Beaux Arts*. In partnership with C. F. Mewès from 1900 he designed such splendid apartments as the public rooms of the Ritz Hotel in London (1906) with its exquisite Louis XVI dining-room. Does one detect a wistful sadness in this wonderful room or is it that one knows it to be the swan-song of an era rather than the opening up of a new tradition for the new century which Simpson and his contemporaries envisaged? When Arthur Davis designed new private rooms such as those in the house at Luton Hoo, originally an Adam house which had passed through calamitous fires and other vicissitudes, he produced interiors which were very like the public rooms of a luxury hotel. The Blue Hall at Luton has precisely this character but when we pass through it into the dining room which, if only by virtue of its single dining table, must have more of the character of a house, we are at once reminded of the dining room at Waddesdon with which we began. They are both marble-lined rooms, the marble forming panelled frames for eighteenth-century Beauvais tapestries – part of a series known as 'Les Beaux Pastorales' and woven between 1775 and 1778 to designs by François Boucher, and an earlier eighteenth-century set 'The Story of the King of China' at Luton. The disconcertingly blank ceiling at Luton may show twentieth-century 'restraint' and

opposite. The library, Biltmore Mansion, near Asheville, North Carolina, USA. Based on the precedent of several castles on the Loire in France, the house was designed by Richard Morris Hunt and built in 1890–5 for William K. Vanderbilt. The scale is huge, and the library in perfect accord with the rest of the building. The ceiling is a large canvas by Tiepolo, bought by the owner from an Italian castle

the glass-panelled doors connecting to the Blue Hall certainly impart to our eyes the hotel atmosphere, but the similarities far outweigh the differences. It is as if the Arts and Crafts, *Art Nouveau* and all the rest had never been. The Luton Hoo rooms are more or less contemporary with Mackintosh who, for all his extraordinary creative powers and apparently progressive outlook, was proceeding into the wilderness. The present lay for a short Indian summer with the British and American Neo-classicists, for they rather than the French or Germans, were the inheritors of the *beaux arts* tradition and of monumental architecture. By about 1890 when he designed 'Chesters' and 'Bryanston', Norman Shaw himself had reached fully fledged Neo-classicism. The first decade of the 1900s was the age of the public building men, T.E.Colcutt, Sir Aston Webb, E.W. Mountford and amongst the younger men at the century's turn such figures as H.V. Lanchester and A.E.Rickards. In 1887, however, the young Edwin Lutyens, then eighteen years old, had become a pupil in the office of Sir Ernest George and so began the greatest architectural career of the second part of our period. He stayed in that office for less than a year and that was the whole of his practical experience before he commenced in practice alone. He greatly admired the work of Philip Webb and Norman Shaw who, rather than Sir Ernest George, are the real influences in his work. In fact from 1897 he worked and lived in a house in Bloomsbury Square which had been Norman Shaw's office. When he took the house Lutyens wrote, 'the house is so delicious. It does for an office so well. First because the first architect of our day used it . . .' and later on 'I believe Norman Shaw is a really great and capable designer, one of the first water. I put him with Wren – really.' Lutyens's early work resembled closely that of Shaw and went, more rapidly, through the same succession of styles commencing with the series of beautiful and Arts and Crafts houses such as 'Munstead Wood' (1896) for Gertrude Jekyll the designer of gardens, 'Orchards' (1899) at Godalming and many others. The principal rooms of these houses were of picturesque forms much in the same way as Shaw's had been, but in the early years of the new century Lutyens became increasingly concerned with English classical and Palladian forms. A real tradition of twentieth-century monumental classical architecture was evolving and for a short time optimism as to the future of such a school seemed justified.

Such a room as the hall at 'Little Thakeham' which dates from 1903 has nothing of the swan-song atmosphere which we persuaded ourselves to see in Arthur Davis's work at the Ritz. This is real forward-looking monumentality. It shows a healthy renaissance-like preoccupation with simple mathematical ratios between the various parts. It is square in section, approximately three cubes long, and divided by the stair screen – itself a fascinating allusion to the medieval screen's passage – in the proportion of three to five. The two openings in the upper walls communicating into the long corridor take their spacing from the axis of the stair compartment and so it all fits together in precise logical sequence. The classical forms are worked out from first principles. This is the spirit of a living tradition and in those seemingly far off days of the great Edwardian houses the classical tradition was coming alive again.

It was not of course to be. The flow of country house projects was drying up. The

The first-class smoking-room of the ship Mauritania, *built in 1907. A luxurious room with details reminiscent of the Italian Renaissance*

beautiful austere geometry of the rooms and corridors of Castle Drogo, building steadily from 1910 to 1930, have all the expression of a young emerging style, but like the great rooms at New Delhi they were built into borrowed time.

Beyond the Great War only those projects which had gathered momentum in earlier years could survive. New Delhi, projecting the ideals of the Edwardian years into the 1920s in this way, was the last great expression of classical monumentality; the loggias, the staircases, the great marble vaults, the marble-lined troughs of water, the colonnades and the state rooms were those of the last 'Temple of Imperial Power'. It is usually suggested that the classical and traditional forms were no longer relevant in the new post-war epoch, but what we witness is not so much the death of an outworn style as the eclipse of monumental architecture itself. In 1880 the search was for a style. By 1920 there was no longer cause for celebration. 'State and grandeur have become irksome to us and are even despised. . . .'

Palazzo Doria, Rome

opposite. One of the suite of rooms decorated at the end of the nineteenth century, and extraordinarily reminiscent of the work of Norman Shaw or T.E. Colcutt in England

Schloss Neuschwanstein, Bavaria

below, left and right. The structure was completed by Georg Dollman in 1880, but work on the interior was still unfinished when Ludwig II abdicated in 1885. The bedroom shown here is in the late Gothic style in contrast to the Romanesque of the other rooms

overleaf. The grey drawing-room at Waddesdon Manor, England: French panelling of about 1740 installed in Baron Ferdinand de Rothschild's house in 1889. In spite of all the furniture and fittings being French eighteenth-century pieces of priceless value, the ensemble has the atmosphere of a sumptuous hotel

Van Eetvelde House, Brussels

left. *This salon was built by Victor Horta in 1895.
This architect's designs are probably the most complete
expression of the style known as Art Nouveau to be
found anywhere in Europe. Especially notable are his
daring use of exposed structural elements, his sure
application of sinuous ornamental forms, and his
originality with functional objects like electric lights*
below left. *Detail of a light fitting from the Van
Eetvelde house*
below right. *Corner of a fireplace in the Van
Eetvelde house*
opposite. *The dining room of the Van Eetvelde house
designed in 1895 by Victor Horta and wonderfully
complete in every detail*

Maxim's Restaurant, Paris

*opposite. This interior, built by Louis Marnez and
Léon Sonnier in 1899, with its sinuous shapes and richness,
lends weight to the theory that the most successful Art Nouveau
interiors were those designed as settings for public eating
right. These doors in Maxim's Restaurant, though now
apparently no longer used, show in the shape of their panels
the whiplash form, so very characteristic of the Art Nouveau
style
below. Léon Sonnier painted the discreet murals in Maxim's
Restaurant in 1899*

Buscot Park, Berkshire, England

opposite. *The Briar Rose room. The house was originally built in 1770 and remains of the first interior may be seen in the ceiling decoration and the cornice. A complete re-decoration was carried out by Sir Ernest George in 1889, and he provided a setting for the Briar Rose paintings by Burne-Jones which were installed in 1890. The furniture is unexpectedly and successfully in the French Empire style*

Palacio Güell, Barcelona

The gallery overlooking the entrance hall, built in 1885–8 by the talented Antoni Gaudí. Moorish affinities are very evident in his early work, whilst later he developed towards his own brand of Art Nouveau

The entrance hall, showing the inventiveness of the work of the architect, not only in his detailing but juxtapositions of spaces

La Vagenende Restaurant, Paris

Another charming example of the success of the Art Nouveau style applied to the decoration of a public restaurant

Detail of the panelling, where dark maghogany contrasts happily with brilliant-cut looking-glass, painted embossed panels and nickel-plated metal

Lloyd's Register of Shipping, London

above. *Ornamental sculpture of the staircase. Beautifully integrated sculpture and architecture is particularly characteristic of the building of this period, and here the balustrade of the stair swells up into a pedestal carrying a symbolic figure in a barque.* opposite. *The General Committee Room. This fine monumental interior was designed by T. E. Colcutt in 1900. The magnificent murals are by Brangwyn*

Leighton House, London

The Arab Hall. Genuine Moorish antique tiles were used in this eminently successful reconstruction which was finished in 1880

Ritz Hotel, London

right. *The dining room, built by Mewés and Davis in 1906. In this delightful room the fanciful interpretation of the Louis XVI style achieves a spirit very close to that of the French eighteenth century*
below. *The Buffet in the dining room*

King Edward VII's Railway Carriage, London

The day compartment of the King's saloon built by the London and North-Western Railway in 1903. The interiors are mostly white with silver-plated beds and fittings, but with no fixed furniture. above, right. Switches in the King's night compartment and a corner of the King's day compartment

Little Thakeham, Sussex, England

The hall in a building designed by Edwin Lutyens in 1903. An almost quintessential interior by this brilliant architect, showing his mastery of the mannerist use of Palladian detail, his extraordinary skill in moulding internal space and his delight in esoteric architectural jokes

MODERN
1920-60

Robert Furneaux Jordan

The first great modern room was really London's Crystal Palace of 1851. It was a very large, temporary but elegant exhibition building, and it had to be erected very quickly. Although a third of a mile long, it was built in a few months; it had to be as easily demolished. It was Paxton who ultimately solved a tough problem by the use of what we would now call 'industrialised' or 'prefabrication' techniques. The Crystal Palace was not the first iron and glass building; the iron bridge at Coalbrookdale had been built over seventy years before. And already in the gardens of prosperous suburban villas were a thousand conservatories. Indeed, it was the Palm House at Kew and the Great Conservatory at Chatsworth that were Paxton's prototypes. Also, and above all, there had been the big English railway stations – Euston, Paddington and the rest.

The Crystal Palace was 'modern' in that it was an 'industrial' building, manufactured by big Midland contractors and then bolted together in Hyde Park. It was also architecture in the highest sense, in that it was inspired by circumstances, deriving design from structure. It stood poised in mid-century – looking back to Regency elegance, forward to 'functionalism' – and its interior was an absolutely integral part of it.

Nothing was ever the same again. Gilbert Scott admitted that there might one day be a wonderful new architecture of iron, symbolic of the age. Ruskin made a similar admission, although he also asked what it was that distinguished architecture from a rat's hole or a railway station. What, however, delayed the emergence of such a new kind of architecture, and even more, of a new kind of interior, was not so much the Crystal Palace, but the things inside it. The Great Exhibition of 1851 was the apotheosis of the Machine Age: a great flood of engines, steam-hammers, mass-produced furniture, ghastly textiles, papiermâché ornament and a tidal wave of gadgets and knick-knacks.

The young William Morris, in his dislike of what he saw, could hardly have been expected to recognise – up there above his head in the iron and the glass – an architecture of a new world. Instead, he employed 'real' craftsmen, working in a 'real' medieval workshop, making furniture, glass and fabrics for a few very rich people. Paradoxically, therefore, this violent reaction against the Crystal Palace and everything in it, this violent

MODERN

reaction against crowded rooms, the upholstery, the ornament and the vulgarity of the Victorian age actually delayed the coming of the good modern room by nearly a century.

Morris, face to face with the Victorian interior, and blind to the potentialities of iron and glass, saw no way out, only a complete rejection of the whole 'cash nexus', of the whole capitalist system, and the substitution of a communist utopia. Morris made superb textiles, massive oak settles and stained glass. The modern interior, however, was something quite different. It had to wait for Frank Lloyd Wright and for Walter Gropius.

Walter Gropius, in spite of his admiration for Morris, had to found the Bauhaus in 1919 in order to train people to design *for* the machine instead of *against* it, a reversal of all that Morris had stood for. Morris thought that what was wrong with Victorian furniture was that it had been made by machinery. But a machine is only a tool, and Gropius knew that what was wrong with Victorian furniture was that it had not been designed to be made by machinery.

Perhaps, coming as Morris did, at the very end of the Gothic Revival, at the end of a century of bogus romanticism, he was born fifty years too soon. He saw his vision of an idealised medieval world so clearly, that in the end he could see the real world only through medieval spectacles. He founded the Arts and Crafts Movement and thereby, for half a century, threw golden Gothic dust in our eyes.

All the same, Morris does mark the frontier between the end of the old order and the beginning of a new. The Victorian room, of almost any class, was the end of something, the rather blowzy end of a High Classic tradition. Wren, Vanbrugh, Kent, Adam, Nash, Barry – these men had made interiors of grandeur or of *grandeur-manqué*: tall windows, rich plaster ceilings, ornate drapery, upholstery and gilded picture frames. Whether well or badly executed, this had, for three centuries, been the English room.

After Philip Webb had built the famous Red House for Morris, after Voysey had built his charming craftsmanlike cottages, after Norman Shaw and the young Lutyens had established their fashionable country house practices, that summary of the typical English interior no longer held good. Not one of these Edwardians was 'modern' or even a pioneer of modernism. They all looked back to the past for their inspiration, but the past they looked to was not that of eighteenth- or nineteenth-century grandeur. It was that of the English vernacular. Whether that vernacular was really suitable to their purpose or not, obsessed as they were with a Morrisian philosophy, they succumbed to its charms; it was after all one of the loveliest vernaculars in the world – that of the English village, manor house, cottage, farm and barn.

If these fashionable architects were a little too free with their leaded lights and their oak beams; if the Garden City was based rather too obviously upon the pattern of the village round the green; and if the mansions they built, with their low rooms, big chimney stacks and cottage casements, were rather absurd as settings for big house parties; it was also true that the Arts and Crafts Movement, with such men as Gimson, Ambrose Heal and Morris to inspire it, had taken a momentous step forward in the history of the English interior. It had all begun as a revolt against the worst horrors of the Great Exhibition and of Victoriana in general. It was all tinged by a romantic yearning

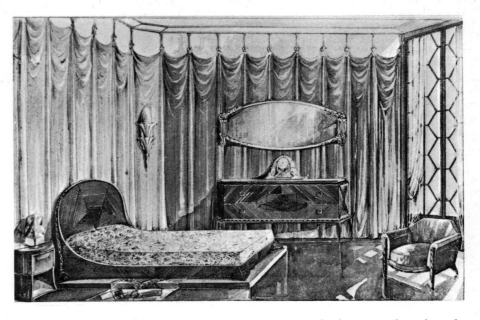

Project for a bedroom with furniture designed by Merlotti, 1928. This furniture still has fairly close affinities with traditional form, as might be expected in Italy. On the other hand a conscious striving after individuality can be seen in some of the details and in the arbitrary disposition of the veneer graining

for medievalism, a hangover from the Gothic Revival involving such things as handmade or even Dutch bricks and tiles, such things as the revival of various crafts and of the English garden. Internally it involved good simple oak furniture – pegged not nailed – fresh spring-like wallpapers and cretonnes, open hearths, bright pottery and a general simplicity of which the nineteenth century had never dreamt.

If Morris's outlook persists anywhere to-day, it is not really among his philosophical disciples within the William Morris Society, but in the craft factories of Holland or Scandinavia. Danish tables and cutlery are part of the ordinary modern interior. The whole attitude inculcated by Morris and by the Arts and Crafts Movement was virtually the main-stream of good interior design until after the First World War, and is not dead now. Nevertheless, it is only one aspect of a very complicated scene. There are others and they may, perhaps, be summarised as: 1 *Art Nouveau* 2 Frank Lloyd Wright and his followers 3 Edwardian grandeur 4 Walter Gropius and the Bauhaus.

Art Nouveau The nineteenth century acknowledged the Ruskinian doctrine that architecture must be ornamented, and indeed that architecture *is* ornamented building. Before the end of the century, however, there were already lively minds who felt that if, through steel and glass, there might be a new architecture, then there must also be a new kind of ornament. That there should be no ornament at all was simply inconceivable. If the Gothic cusps and fretwork must be eliminated then something must be put in their place. What?

It was the Belgian architect, Horta, who said that the lines of ornament could be devised to express such emotions as sorrow, joy or lassitude. Steel, being ductile, lent itself admirably to this dubious theory. And so, in the end, we had all those strange, whirling, swooning lines of *art nouveau*. It is a phase of art that is remembered best, perhaps, not in architecture but in *The Yellow Book* and in Beardsley's drawings. In furniture and decoration one thinks of the high-backed chairs and the beaten copper and the attenuated lilies. The debt of *art nouveau* to Swinburne and Rosetti and Walter Pater is too obvious to need stressing. As an art, for all its affectations, it had its high moments. In Chicago, in the 1890s, Louis Sullivan, the 'inventor' of the skyscraper, devised in steel some very rich and very complex ornaments of great beauty. In Spain, at the beginning of this century, Gaudí had already realised that concrete, being a poured or moulded material, could also be a manifestation of *art nouveau*. Combining rubble, concrete and polychromatic tiles, Gaudí made Barcelona into something of a pilgrimage city for modern architects. His was a grotesque, sinuous, exotic and occasionally megalomaniac style. It gave to Barcelona flats, mansions and the splendid *Sagrada Familia*. Unfortunately the single individual room comes very little into the Gaudí picture. Another master of *art nouveau* was Charles Rennie Mackintosh of Glasgow. If many of the more playful fantasies of *art nouveau* are to be found in his domestic interiors and in the famous scintillating Glasgow tea-shops – almost great rooms in their own right – his Glasgow Art School managed to be both a fine essay in *art nouveau* and a fine piece of early functionalism. Its library may be considered one of the first truly great interiors of the twentieth century. It is rich and entirely original, depending, as it does, upon its architecture for its decoration, not upon added 'art'. It looks forward, not back.

Frank Lloyd Wright and his followers   When Louis Sullivan was designing those very first skyscrapers in Chicago, he already had at his elbow the young Frank Lloyd Wright, destined to be the most brilliant and the most sensational architect of this century. Wright was, in his life and work and mien, one of the most romantic men who ever lived. He had soaked himself in Victor Hugo and William Morris and John Ruskin, not to mention Shelley and Wordsworth, whose pantheism he shared. Yet there he was, an architect in the rich, roaring Chicago of the 1890s, – a traditionalist without a tradition. Small wonder that with Walt Whitman he turned his back on Europe and on the whole of America's second-hand *Ecole des Beaux Arts* attitudes. With Whitman he looked west to discover an American vernacular. He discovered instead the soil, the granite and the pine. At the same time he gloried in the whole modern world of locomotives, steamships and steel. It was out of all that that he evolved his 'organic architecture': 'you don't put a house on a hill, it grows there'. His rooms were big and low, with huge hearths and great leather-cushioned window-seats and massive oak furniture, as massive as Morris's but not Gothic. If anything there might be a touch of *art nouveau*, but any actual

Water-colour by William Walcot of the design for the ballroom at Government House, Delhi, 1924. The final flowering of the 'British Raj' style can be seen here, grand, esoteric, oddly unconvincing, yet at the same time rather impressive

imported elements tended to be oriental rather than European. The living-room of the early Robie House, 1909, or still more that of the Kaufmann House at Bear Run, Pennsylvania, with its concrete balconies projecting out over the water-falls in the birch forest, are among the great rooms of all time. They are also the perfect marriage of high romanticism and the structural techniques of our own time. Almost certainly, too, the large general office of the Johnson Wax Building at Racine, with its tall, almost Mycenean mushroom columns and its clearstory of tubular lights, is another landmark in the history of the interior. To those who think that modern building, just because it uses glass and steel, is necessarily arid and unromantic, these interiors of Wright are a tremendous answer.

Edwardian grandeur   This is, perhaps, a rather misleading term for the interiors created in the years before the Second World War; it has to cover such a multitude of sins and so few glories. The further debasement and extension of the Classical tradition from the Victorian era into our own century offers very little that is worthwhile. In the earlier Edwardian epoch there were a few deliberate *tours-de-force* in lushness: the scarlet and white suites of Mewès and Davis's Ritz, the gilded and mirrored baroque of the Café Royal Grill in London, and then later, the occasional Lutyens banking hall. But what else? If there are any fine interiors of this brief era of grandeur then surely they come, like the houses of which they are part, from the fashionable practices of men like Norman Shaw, C.F.A. Voysey, Edwin Lutyens or half-a-dozen lesser men such as Baillie Scott or Philip Tilden, whose names are, on the whole, forgotten.

The young Lutyens was rather different. Genius or not, what he did he nearly always did superbly. The Morris tradition had created a very curious phenomenon – a middle and an upper-middle class of taste, if not always of knowledge. It was a taste based upon the vernacular, and in England a whole class filled with admiration for the thatched hovels of their grandfathers' tenants. All this, at its worst, created an absurd cult of 'ye olde'. But this taste also gave rise to the week-end cottage, the amateur gardener, the antique collector and possibly some of the most comfortable and 'gracious' homes ever built. For fine creative artists such as Norman Shaw or Edwin Lutyens, or even for the more commonplace designers of such things as suburban 'stockbroker's Tudor', it created a dilemma, the dilemma of building large houses to resemble old cottages, a phenomenon that was common to many countries. A Norman Shaw house such as Cragside in Northumberland or Leys Wood in Surrey – taken wing by wing – offer a series of charming pastiche vignettes, each complete with leaded casements, dormer windows and chimney-stack. Take the house as a whole, with its thirty-odd bedrooms, and the thing was an absurdity.

Lutyens was a greater master than Shaw. For his partner in garden design, Gertrude Jekyll, he built a house at Munstead with a great stone and brick hearth where hang all the bellows, spits and cauldrons that no one was ever meant to use, and perhaps to the end Lutyens' restorations of the very old constituted his best interiors. In his vernacular work he handled his oak, plaster and iron better than any of his imitators, but at Marshcourt in Hampshire he tried to face the absurdly impossible problem: he built a 'Tudorbethan' mansion and fitted Palladian rooms inside it. In spite of gimmicks, such as a billiards table made out of one piece of chalk and a nursery that was circular so that no children could be put in the corner, there were the great moments. There is the corridor here, the kitchen there, the library somewhere else, but there is probably not one that can be counted amongst the world's really great rooms.

Walter Gropius   A thousand everyday things, seemly and decent in design – our telephones, typewriters, books, mugs and chairs – are often a little better than they might have been because of Gropius and 'the Bauhaus Idea'. 'The Bauhaus', said Mies van der Rohe, who succeeded Gropius in the vanguard of architecture, 'was not an institution with a clear programme – it was an idea, and Gropius formulated that idea with great precision.' As early as 1911 Gropius had caused something of a sensation with his design for the Fagus Factory and for his 1914 building at the Cologne Werkbund Exhibition – clear engineering structures in glass and steel, stripped of all stylistic irrelevancies.

In the Weimar Bauhaus, in 1919, Gropius became director of one of the best equipped art schools in the world. He also became the symbol of a cause. The price had to be paid. The Bauhaus, with its explosive ideas in design, attracted individualists such as Reinhardt, Kokoschka, Kandinsky, Chagall, Klee, Mies van der Rohe, Breuer, Moholy Nagy. The Bauhaus became in fact, most emphatically, *avant-garde*. And that was more than the bourgeoisie of Weimar could stand. In the new 1925 Bauhaus at Dessau, Gropius brought one era to an end and opened another. Morris had been a Luddite: destroy the machines not only because they make ugly things but because they make unhappy men. Gropius said, understand the machine, design things that it can make well, and a new world opens before you. Every student had his own mechanic-instructor and his own artist-instructor. Furniture, pottery, metal work, typography, graphic art, theatre art, fashion and so on had each a department with workshops. Architecture was not taught but architecture was 'always in the air', everything was related to it. No single artist or institution has ever altered the interiors of the world in the same way as the Bauhaus, not at any rate if we consider its influence and the dissemination of its ideas and personnel over half a century. For a modern art or technical college to have first-class machinery and equipment is now a commonplace; the idea was born in the Bauhaus. The Bauhaus, as 'a bacillus of Jewish-Bolshevik infection' (Goering's words), was duly closed by Goebbels, or rather, it closed itself rather than compromise with evil. Gropius, Mies van der Rohe, Breuer have been not least among modern architects and designers in the United States.

So the threads come together, the rather diverse ancestry of the modern interior – the Gothic Revival, the Railway Age, the Arts and Crafts Movement, *art nouveau*, Frank Lloyd Wright, Edwardian grandeur, the Bauhaus. Some great interiors clearly owe more to one of these antecedents than to the others; none is independent of them all.

In the twenties all the world was going to Stockholm. Sweden, after the seclusion of its neutrality in the First World War, was being 'discovered'. The principal objective of these travellers was a pilgrimage to the new Town Hall on the shores of Stockholm Harbour. What was peculiar about the tourist flood was that this very accomplished

building was thought to be 'modern'. Some even pretended to be a little shocked at its modernism or to take credit for being so advanced as not to be shocked. In view of what was happening elsewhere in the world, in places as far apart as Vienna and Chicago, this was remarkable.

It has been said that the English Arts and Crafts Movement, perhaps because the soil of industrial England was unkind, found a surer home in the Scandinavian countries, small, cosy, bourgeois and materially civilised, as well as being possessed of long craft traditions that industrialism had never quite killed. Of that movement, the Town Hall at Stockholm was therefore something of an apotheosis. Of course it was very Swedish too, not only in such obviously Baltic things as the handling of the *campanile* and the little onion domes, but in its marvellously full exploitation of beautiful materials – wood, brick, granite, green marble. These northern countries are lands of great workmen. The Town Hall at Stockholm does not, like Gropius's buildings of the same decade, strip itself of all stylistic irrelevancies; on the contrary it transposes the arcades of the Doge's Palace from the Adriatic to the Baltic. They may suffer a sea-change in the process, becoming brick instead of stone, but the debt of Stockholm to Venice is very evident. To architectural progress Stockholm Town Hall made no contribution whatsoever. But in the artistry and craftsmanship, the decoration and furnishing of its interior, it gave to our century more than one truly great interior.

Now, the essence of this kind of craftsmanship, whether or not it relies upon actual forms taken from the past, is to use the *materials* of the past, and to use them with all the integrity and skill and understanding of great craftsmanship. This may be neither an acceptance nor an exploitation of the modern world in Gropius's sense, but it is not an ignoble ideal. It may give great joy. Moreover, in the earlier years of the twentieth century, and Stockholm Town Hall was being designed during the First World War, it went about as far as anyone just short of genius could be expected to go.

In the Golden Hall, the great banqueting room of the Town Hall, we have a master-piece of its kind. The main decorative material is gold mosaic, with great dim figures looming out of the gold. The hall is planned with a series of huge curved niches, running the full height of the room, around and into which, in its true function as a covering material, the mosaic sweeps. These big niches take the place, as it were, of the Byzantine domes for which mosaic was originally devised. Like those domes their curves cause the

263

MODERN

mosaic to catch the light, to glitter a little in the impressive gloom and the glow of candles. The gloom, the big low banqueting tables and the carved stools, make this banqueting hall, although it is in truth only for city councillors, a place fit for the Norse gods. It is positively Odinesque.

In the other rooms of this Town Hall we have something less dramatic, but no less well done. There is, for instance, the long Princes' Gallery looking over the harbour, with its richly moulded window jambs and crystal chandeliers. There is also the so-called 'Blue Hall', a fine piece of cut-brick craftsmanship with marble stair and gallery of great beauty; there is a continuous clerestory window which makes the ceiling look as if it were suspended from heaven.

The Stockholm Town Hall, designed by Ragnar Östberg, was of course the central building of what has come to be called 'the Swedish Renaissance'. In addition to Östberg one must also remember Ivar Tengbom, whose Högalids Church and Stockholm Concert Hall are among the more remarkable interiors of this century. The church was in the same 'craft' tradition as the Town Hall, with touches of Lutheran baroque in an otherwise extraordinarily chaste interior. The Concert Hall is a delicate, elegant building with a fine attenuated portico externally, and with a proscenium which is a most curious Classical pastiche, a rather brilliant piece of neo-Grec, or counterpart of several mediocre English attempts to 'go Regency' at about that time. The smaller concert room, an integral part of the main Concert Hall building, is rich with swirling murals and ceiling patterns and must certainly rank high among our great rooms. It must, for instance, rank higher than Rex Whistler's Dining Room at Plas Newydd or his restaurant at the Tate, although Whistler must not be forgotten in any survey of rooms of this period. Also in the delicate and classical style of the Swedish interior must be placed several works by Sweden's most distinguished modern architect, Gunnar Asplund, notably the very Grecian interior of the City Library, the rather Etruscan promenade of the Skandia Cinema, and the two chapels of Asplund's great Crematorium.

Very little later in date than the Stockholm Town Hall, very similar in function and, therefore, directly comparable, is the Town Hall at Hilversum in Holland. It was designed by W. M. Dudok in the late 1920s. This building is surrounded by the landscape and flowers of a garden city. It is a direct and simple piece of Dutch brickwork. Its simplicity is deceptive. It seems to belong to the clean and domestic world of Dutch suburbia, a rather larger version of one of Dudok's Hilversum schools, which really set the tune for so many modern schools all over the world. In fact this Town Hall owes a lot of its quality to Frank Lloyd Wright. He had come just a generation too soon to display, Miesian fashion, his naked steel and glass as being in itself the whole of his theme. He welcomed steel and concrete, as at Bear Run or Racine, because they enabled him through the creation of big spans, cantilevered masses and deep shadows, to make what was already romantic even more so, to design from his heart while being also a man of his time. If this was true of Frank Lloyd Wright, in Pennsylvania birch forests, it was also true of Dudok in the much simpler world of a Dutch township.

Internally the Town Hall at Hilversum is almost a laboratory specimen of our various

sources of modern design. In its general picturesqueness, its contrast of high and low spaces, and its use of raw brick, tiles and timber, it is highly romantic. In the high-backed ebony chairs, the elongated decoration and clustered light fittings, it is curiously dated; it is surprising how much it owes, directly or indirectly, to *art nouveau* and Mackintosh and Voysey. The finest room in this building, in a very simple but very elegant Dutch manner, is the Civil Marriage Room, perhaps one of the best of the great rooms of the rather arid years when it was built.

In the years before World War II, when Wright, Gropius and Le Corbusier were already world figures, the English scene was not inspiring. A few men, such as Wells Coates or Lubetkin, did initiate the modern interior: there was Lubetkin's own remarkable pent-house flat at Highpoint, Highgate, but on the whole the opportunities were just not there. The wrong sort of architects had the wrong sort of patrons. Among them, however, Howard Robertson achieved something fairly memorable in the big parabolic concrete roof at the Horticultural Hall in Westminster, even if it was only a memory of the Gothenburg Exhibition a few years before. Other interiors by the same architect, such as the Berkeley Buttery with its modish 'gas-pipe' furniture and newly-discovered tartan, were products of fashion. They were no more important than current women's clothes.

One had the right to expect rather more of the new Portland Place headquarters of the Royal Institute of British Architects in 1934. Alas, glamorous as all the glitter may have seemed at the time, all those current clichés of 'empire woods' and engraved glass were, even then, more suitable for a smartly sedate restaurant than for a learned society. Lutyens maliciously dismissed it as the 'Portland Plaza'. Actually, however, Grey Wornum reminds us, with his brilliant plan and section, that a great room is something more than decoration. If basic proportions are wrong, then no mere 'decorator' can save the situation.

Modern architecture never fully emancipated itself from an irrelevant past until, as in the last twenty years, it began to understand its own 'pre-history' – Victorian engineering and the implications thereof. Of all our sources of modern design that is the most

MODERN

important. Of course there is no recognisable Victorian engineering in modern architecture; it has been a case of evolution, not imitation. There is no palpable Roman engineering in Gothic cathedrals. In both cases the line of derivation can be easily traced, but there has also been a gradual transmutation from one into quite another architecture.

True, it is now over sixty years since Frank Lloyd Wright proclaimed the doctrine that the modern world must be accepted if art is to survive. True, also, that it is nearly forty years since Le Corbusier, in *Vers une architecture*, proclaimed the doctrine that we must look for inspiration not to the masterpieces of the past, but to those of the present, which are ships, silos and locomotives; longer still since Van der Velde said that 'the engineers are our Hellenes'. All easy to say, more difficult to do. Only, indeed, when the doctrine had been understood and acted upon, only when design was derived from, rather than imposed upon, structure, did the young architect find himself going beyond the purely nominal functionalism of his predecessors and turning structural necessity into art.

Modern structure can be divided into two quite separate developments, although both depend upon steel. One is the steel frame infilled with glass or opaque panels; the other is the use of steel in the form of rods or mesh buried in concrete so that it may be less massive than when it was used in ancient Rome. Aesthetically these two systems finally emerge as contrasted systems, although both revolutionised the interior. The first, the steel frame, is a rigidly disciplined system such as the Greeks would have admired; it is an arrangement of rectangles giving a form of decoration dependent mainly upon simple geometric relationships and upon marvellous potentialities of light and space. The second system, reinforced concrete, enables the designer to create almost any shape he chooses; it is virtually a plastic material, capable of as great a textural richness as any of the historic styles, and of the dramatic enclosure of space in forms that go far beyond the dreams of the Baroque artists: vaults, domes, shells of vast size and great lightness, so that a hundred-foot-high dome three inches thick is an easy reality. Both these systems have their masters. Mies van der Rohe of the earlier generation, and Arne Jacobsen of the younger, have explored the steel frame; while Le Corbusier in France, Luigi Nervi in Italy and Jutzen in Australia have realised, in their different ways, the possibilities of reinforced concrete and provided a series of great interiors.

below left. Design for a dining room by Leleu from L'Illustration, 1933: *a sophisticated project by one of the 'grands décorateurs' of the day*

below right. Design for a bathroom for 'Mrs K. in the United States', unnecessarily wasteful in space. The date of this design is 1933

Taking the steel frame first, one must forget its most obvious manifestation, which is the typical office block, all over the world, bought by the yard. The two constituents of the steel frame building, the rectangularity and the transparency, are in fact capable of achieving a splendid, if simple, beauty. It is over ten years now since Mies van der Rohe designed the Farnsworth House, near Chicago. This design ironed out all the complexities that have gathered round the very word 'house' and reduced them to a single fine unity. To those who dislike it, the Farnsworth House, and the Philip Johnson House after it, was no more than a glass box. It was, however, an extremely sophisticated glass box, both aesthetically and technically. It was something that was designed with the supreme virtuosity of a Ming pot. All the mechanics of this house, plumbing, cooking, and so on being contained within a central spine, all that remains is, quite simply, space – an interior. This is indeed a great room, all the more so because in any usual sense of the word it is completely undecorated. It is in itself its own decoration; there is nothing added. It proclaims its architect's famous aphorism that 'less is more'. The room's steel outline encloses a most careful series of proportions. All the rest is glass, through which can be seen the spring green, autumn red or snowclad North American foliage. Here is the full exploitation of techniques – built-in services, double-glazing, welded steel, air conditioning – and all in the service of art. This is the marriage with nature no less than Frank Lloyd Wright's 'organic architecture' and no less than the Parthenon when it was set upon its platform so that it could never be seen except against the sky. Internally the simplest possible arrangement of a little of the simplest possible furniture is in strict geometric relationship to the enclosing structure. A Japanese may well understand this kind of interior better than a European. It is as rarified as it is beautiful. It is stark poetry, but poetry nevertheless.

The Farnsworth House must stand in its own right as one example of the steel-framed interior, the great room undecorated. Mention must also be made of Mies's architectural studios in Crown Hall, Illinois Institute of Technology, Chicago, and of the hall of his Ricardi Offices in Mexico City; also of the main room of Kinoryu Kikutake's Sky House in Japan, and of the glittering staircase in Arne Jacobsen's Town Hall at Rodovre in Denmark, or his Dining Hall at St. Catherine's College, Oxford. They all come in the same category of buildings which derive their decoration from their structure.

In the plastic qualities and textural richness, as well as in the structural possibilities, of reinforced concrete we have a different and indeed a contrasted system. In the Unity Church at Oak Park, Illinois, in 1906, Frank Lloyd Wright built the first 'monolithic' concrete building. Inevitably perhaps, at that date he could not realise the material's true potential; the exterior and the interior of this church are ingenious but also heavy, almost Egyptian in character, whereas in fact the material is capable of the very greatest delicacy and flexibility. We come much nearer the mark in the magnificent interior of Auguste Perret's church at Le Raincy of 1922, where he has shown how the artist in reinforced concrete can rival and perhaps excel the old medieval builders of 'lantern' churches. The walls of Le Raincy are concrete grilles filled with stained glass. As at Ste Chapelle or King's College Chapel one is within a coloured lantern.

above left. *In this room designed by the Englishman Gordon Russell for Prince Chirasakti in 1940, the mirror glass, the chromium plate, the veneered ply, the 'modernistic' pattern fabrics are all brought together to make up an interior of quiet charm*
above right. *A living room in the 'Maison Clarté', Geneva, built by Le Corbusier in 1932. A very good example of the best design of this period: a straightforward conception of clean shapes, with excellent furniture designed by Le Corbusier and Charlotte Périand*

opposite. *The dining room at Plas Newydd, Wales, with murals painted by the gifted Rex Whistler during the late 1930s. Whistler was a decorator and illustrator with a remarkably strong sense of architecture and in these murals he achieved great spontaneity*

It was Le Corbusier who, from the beginning and apart altogether from his social and town-planning theories, always realised that in reinforced concrete he had a wonderful new medium. He was concerned so much with the design of his building as a sculptural thing in the landscape that he was not really, except incidentally, the creator of great interiors, although here and there they seemed to happen.

Nearly forty years ago, in the famous villa at Garches, he did create what might be called the first of the truly modern interiors. Practising what he had preached in *Vers une architecture* he did, as if the interior were the bridge of a ship, take the long windows round almost the whole perimeter of the room, and he did, practising what he had preached in *Ville Radieuse*, lift the main room to first-floor level so that the windows were among the foliage. It is naïve now, but at the time it was the design of a total space in relation, as in Mies van der Rohe's Farnsworth House, to the world outside.

Towards the end of Le Corbusier's life he built in all humility the little pilgrim church at Ronchamp, which is curiously reminiscent of some small Byzantine chapel on an Aegean island. Its whole technique lies in the use of concrete as a *poured* material, the marks of the wooden shuttering left untouched, the walls thick, massive and rounded. The windows, like the little windows in the massive domes of Byzantium, emphasise this structural weight. In contrast with the glass walls of steel framed buildings, the Miesian technique, these windows are tiny punched holes spaced almost at random over the wall surface. Filled with stained glass they softly tint the simple white walls within and make of Ronchamp Le Corbusier's one great interior.

Other designers have gone farther than Le Corbusier in the more obviously decorative and sculptural aspects of reinforced concrete, as well as in the actual shaping of the structure itself. Reinforced concrete enables us to return to the dynamic of the Baroque, only more so.

In the new city of Brasilia, based upon Lucio Costa's master plan, the architect Oscar Niemeyer has created a very remarkable group of civic buildings, and also one great interior. The main hall of the President's Palace combines the two basic forms of modern structure. Viewed from within it is purely Miesian: a lovely cage of steel and glass enclosing a sweep of empty marble floor. Through the slightly greenish glass one glimpses the surrounding verandah with its subtle but rather Baroque reinforced concrete columns.

The Italian engineer Luigi Nervi is said in his lifetime to have gone through the same development, *mutatis mutandis*, as the Gothic builders went through in four centuries, from the weight of Romanesque to the fretted complexities of Tudor vaults. Perhaps a stadium for the Olympic Games in Rome, or a big skating rink, can hardly be called 'rooms' but the fact that Nervi has taken to the limit these delicate networks of fine concrete ribs, spanning large areas, is surely something that must affect the rooms of the future. Four walls and a ceiling, however splendidly painted or panelled, is only one kind of room. Modern structure, like medieval vaulting, suggests other, and almost unlimited possibilities.

The mere reticulation of the surface of a building, however, affects the rooms inside very little. Saarinen's US Embassy in London is an example. On the other hand, when the architect once manages to leave behind him all the rectangles so easily created on the drawing-board, and to leave behind him the habits of thought of a thousand years, then even the parallel with medieval or Baroque architecture may become quite inadequate. Almost any shaped volume of space may be enclosed. Buckminster Fuller's geostatic domes – he claims that he could put all New York City under a dome – or Saarinen's TWA Building at Kennedy Airport, with its huge wing-shaped concourse, are only a hint of what may be the future of the interior. In the new architecture all shapes are possible, and we have only begun to realise it.

below left. *Picture gallery in the Palazzo Bianco, Genoa, Italy, 1952. The Italians led the landslide of modern design towards elegance in the 1950s, and this is another example of their skill in combining new and old*
below right. *Drawing of the entrance from the lower to the upper foyer, Hotel Leofric, Coventry, England, 1955, particularly expressive of the feeling of English design in the mid-50s*

Skandia Cinema, Stockholm

Designed by the great Swedish architect Gunnar Asplund and built in 1922–3, this delightful auditorium amply bears out the contention that 'great' interiors are now almost entirely in the field of public rather than private architecture

opposite. The lower promenade, another brilliant interior by Asplund, quite worthy of a place in the catalogue of great galleries of the past

Town Hall, Hilversum, Holland

opposite. *The Council room, designed by W. M. Dudok in 1930. As in the marriage room, a great number of the favourite details of the 1920s and 30s were first designed by this original Dutch architect*

Villa at Garches, Seine et Oise, France

This very famous interior, designed in 1926 by Le Corbusier, the architect who has probably had the most influence in Europe over the last forty years, shows almost all the elements which made him famous – the open plan, the large areas of window, the frame structure, the architectural built-in furniture

City library, Stockholm

The librarian's office, designed by Gunnar Asplund in 1928. Intimate and domestic, but the design of the furniture and decoration has the elegant genius which distinguishes this architect's work

Plas Newydd,
Anglesea, Wales

Rex Whistler painted the murals of this dining room during the years 1936–40 and he created a unique but costly room whose only popular parallel could be found in the pictorial wall-papers of the early nineteenth century

Philip Johnson's house, New Canaan, Connecticut, USA

The guest bedroom in the house built for himself by Philip Johnson in 1949. Constructed after the main part of the house, this room demonstrates his re-awakening interest in the more traditional approach to the assembly of architectural elements

St Catherine's College, Oxford, England

The dining hall, built between 1960 and 1964. The designer of this highly successful building was the Dane Arne Jacobsen, and this room displays a sophisticated austerity wholly appropriate for an establishment of learning

Time-Life building, London

opposite. *The Director's dining room, built in 1953. A number of architects and designers were employed on the interiors of this office building, and the result is an intriguing cross-section of the English design world. Leonard Manasseh and Partners achieved a curious idiosyncratic charm with this room, and some of the details, unexpectedly, show 'Arts & Crafts' characteristics*
below. *The Conference Room. The architect of this room was H. T. Cadbury-Brown*

Johnson Wax building, Racine, Wisconsin, USA

*Built by Frank Lloyd Wright in 1938–9. The ranks of mushroom columns, the formality of the arrangement
of the specially designed furniture, and the noble scale make this a truly great interior*

Royal Institute of British Architects, London

opposite. *The entrance of the Henry Florence Room. This building, built by G. Grey Wornum in 1934, is an
absolute museum of what might be called the 'later George V style'. Empire woods, native marbles, phosphor
bronze and sand-blasted glass all make up an ambiance which is slightly dowdy but very assured. The bust is of
the late H. S. Goodhart-Rendell*

Falling Water, Pennsylvania, USA

Completed in 1937 by Frank Lloyd Wright, this is perhaps his most famous house. The main room exhibits a number of his well-known trade marks – the low ceiling emphasising the great width and broad glass area, the exposed natural materials, the unusual modelling of some of the surfaces

A house in Hampton, Connecticut, USA

Another highly sophisticated 'non-architecture' room, with a sunk sitting area in the middle of the marble floor. The house was built by Eero Saarinen in 1957

Taliesin, Spring Green, Wisconsin, USA

*Designed in 1911 but subsequently much altered, it was always Frank Lloyd Wright's principal residence.
Various levels are cleverly used, and natural materials, unadorned, are much in evidence. The master's hat and
stick may be noted, carefully placed on the table in the foreground*

Taliesin West, Phoenix, Arizona, USA

The winter residence built for himself by Frank Lloyd Wright. The building began in 1938 and went on for many years. Materials were rough local stone and dark timber, with canvas panels disposed to allow through ventilation, and as always with this architect, the handling is masterly

ACKNOWLEDGEMENTS

The Editor and publishers wish to express their thanks to Edwin Smith for taking the majority of photographs for the book, and to the owners of all the interiors photographed for their co-operation. They are also grateful to the individuals or institutions mentioned below for supplying the additional photographs and illustrations or for reproduction permissions, and to H. Lionel Williams for his assistance with the American pictures. The illustrations are identified by the page on which they appear.

p. 15, *left and right*: Royal Institute of British Architects (RIBA); p. 21: reproduced by gracious permission of HM The Queen; p. 23: RIBA; p. 25: A. C. Cooper Ltd; p. 31, *left and right*: RIBA; p. 32: RIBA; p. 33: Photo Anderson; pp. 46, 47: reproduced by gracious permission of HM The Queen; pp. 61, 62, 63: RIBA; p. 67: RIBA; p. 69: RIBA; p. 82: Colonial Williamsburg, USA; p. 103: reproduced by gracious permission of HM The Queen; p. 105: Photographie Bulloz; pp. 106, 107: RIBA; p. 113: RIBA; p. 115, *above and below*: RIBA; p. 118: M. E. Warren (Photography); p. 139: The Smithsonian Institution, National Gallery of Art, Washington; p. 191 *top left and right and below*: RIBA; pp. 149, 150: RIBA; p. 153: RIBA; p. 158, *above and below*: Ezra Stoller Associates; p. 159, *above left and right*: Central Office of Information, Poland; pp. 160–1: Colin Jones; p. 173: Ezra Stoller Associates; pp. 178, 179: RIBA; p. 181, *left*: RIBA; p. 183: M. Newman Ltd; p. 189: Freer Gallery of Art, Washington; p. 190: RIBA; p. 192: RIBA; p. 193: The Brooklyn Museum; pp. 194–5: Freer Gallery of Art, Washington; p. 199 *below*: Missouri Historical Society; p. 202: The Brooklyn Museum; p. 203: Ezra Stoller Associates; p. 206–7: reproduced by courtesy of the Museum of British Transport; p. 213: Lennart Olson; p. 218: RIBA; p. 221: *Architect and Building News* (RIBA); p. 223: *Building* (RIBA); p. 225: RIBA; p. 226: RIBA; p. 228: *L'Art 1900* (Art et Métiers Graphiques); p. 229: RIBA; p. 233: reproduced by courtesy of the National Trust, Waddesdon Manor; p. 234: Biltmore Estate, USA; p. 237: Cunard Ltd; p. 240–1: reproduced by courtesy of the National Trust, Waddesdon Manor; p. 254: reproduced by courtesy of the Museum of British Transport; p. 259: *La Casabella* (RIBA); p. 260: *Architectural Review* (RIBA); p. 263 *left*: *Building* (RIBA); p. 263 *right*: *Architectural Review* (RIBA); p. 265 *left*: *La Casabella* (RIBA); p. 265 *right*: *Architectural Review* (RIBA); p. 266 *left and right*: *L'Illustration*; p. 268 *left*: *Architectural Review* (RIBA); p. 268 *right*: *Architecture d'Aujourd'hui* (RIBA); p. 271 *left*: *Domus* (RIBA); p. 271 *right*: *Architectural Review* (RIBA); p. 282: Ezra Stoller Associates, by courtesy of Johnson Wax; pp. 284, 5, 6, 7: Ezra Stoller Associates.